"This thrilling book takes us into the heart of one of the most powerful spiritual places on Earth—Zanskar. It is a must read for all those who love and recognize the healing power of place and the adventure that spiritual travel can open up."

—**Andrew Harvey**, author of
The Hope and *Journey In Ladakh*

"This is a beautiful book for every woman who has ever wanted to do something extraordinary. Amy's solo trek through the Himalayas is an inspiration for all of us who know deep down that we are capable of so much more. Reading her story is sure to light a fire within you to expand your own horizons and tap into untold dimensions of inner strength, courage, determination and resilience."

—**Claire Zammit**, Ph.D., Founder,
FemininePower.com

"For those pulled by both a spiritual heart and an inquiring mind, Adventure in Zanskar will reaffirm your search for Truth. Amy provides a unique window into the beauty and wisdom of a timeless Buddhist culture that inspires us to believe and know that it is possible for us, as a human family, to live in harmony and happiness. It's an inspiring story and example we all need!"

—**Sadhvi Bhagawati Saraswati**,
President of the Divine Shakti Foundation, author of
From Hollywood to the Himalayas

ADVENTURE IN ZANSKAR

A young woman's solitary journey to
reach physical and metaphysical heights

AMY EDELSTEIN

Emergence Education Press • Philadelphia

Adventure In Zanskar
By Amy Edelstein

Copyright © 2021 Amy Edelstein

ISBN: 978-1-7352650-8-7

Library of Congress Control Number: 2021918181

Published in the United States of America by:
Emergence Education Press
622 S. 4th Street, Ste., 63767
Philadelphia, PA 19147
www.EmergenceEducation.com

For more on the Amy Edelstein
and her educational nonprofit:
www.TheConsciousClassroom.com
www.InnerStrengthEducation.org

Printed & bound in the United States of America

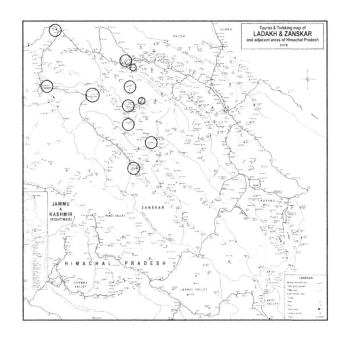

With deep love and gratitude to the people of Zanskar, who opened their homes to me and gave me a pearl of inestimable price—the experience of harmony on earth.

To all the great teachers who planted seeds of wisdom as freely as wildflowers sow their seeds on the back of the wind, I bow to you and thank you for your practice, patience, and passion to liberate all beings.

TABLE OF CONTENTS

Prologue

Sometimes we do things in our lives that, as important as they seem at the time, only vibrate with that special magic decades later. Not because we dwell on those memories that much, but because the artifacts from those events are the only things we have left. My adventure in Zanskar is one of those.

I have kept a journal pretty much ever since I could write. At eight years old, I wrote philosophically about the death of my blue parakeet Tuki, contemplating how all things die, that I would also die, and that death was and always will be just as much a part of life as living. I kept my journals; in fact, I kept virtually every scrap of paper I wrote on until I was thirty, when I threw most of them away in an impulsive act meant to show my detachment from the past and my commitment to the eternal now. In that ill-advised purge went meticulous notes I took during from teachings with some of the great masters of the late twentieth century in Tibetan Buddhism, Theravada Buddhism, Vedanta, Hatha Yoga, and ascetic yoga. It included accounts of the great Khumbh Mela of 1986 in Haridwar, where somewhere between three- and eleven-million mahatmas, fakirs, pilgrims, seekers, and a good share of spiritual charlatans gathered for a month-long pilgrimage with sights and meetings that read like a fantastical tale from *The Arabian Nights*. I tossed accounts from late second-wave radical feminist gatherings and anti-nuclear organizing in 1980 in Ithaca, NY, journals scribbled in boxcars while jumping freight trains across America, reading (but of course) Jack Kerouac's *The Dharma Bums*. Unceremoniously discarded were poems labored over in the middle of the night after seeing Seamus Heaney read, others written after a poets' party where Allen Ginsburg tried to pick up my boyfriend. His reading, harmonium included, was far more egoic and far less inspiring than Heaney's, truth be told.

Gone were page after page where I negotiated the insights from hallucinogenic substances and jam music, my own version of William James' experiments. I was pondering the purpose of life, and more specifically, the purpose of *my* life. Themes therein were always about bettering the world, alleviating suffering, finding deeper meaning, and wrestling with the demons of self-doubt and pride. Trying to find meaning in a postmodern world, in a mid-west-ish industrial city, where beer and football, steel and immigrants formed the backbone of the town. My journals were also always about going on adventures and quests to realize and to prove that I could do anything a man could, like working on an oil rig in Sidney, Montana at 125lbs next to 250lb crewmates. Anything to break free from the invisible chains, inside and out, that were keeping me bound and limited, all the while my culture was telling me that I was free. Pages of my neat longhand included descriptions of magic Greek seas with fluorescent algae that shimmered in the moonlight when I waved my arm through the water, descriptions of beautiful Burmese women who smiled beneath sandalwood paste, and ponderings of the loneliness growing up in an environment that didn't know much about the ley lines of spiritual transformation. I tossed big black trash bags full of my writings, all in one rash and unhappy act.

But surviving that purge was one small Indian copybook, the kind children use in school, filled with tiny economical handwriting, vocabulary lists, guest house addresses and the names of teachers I'd heard about and wanted to meet. It contained observations and contemplations from one of my treks, when I'd set off, alone, in search of harmony in the high Himalayas. The journal had been carefully protected in a hardback goldenrod-colored folder I had picked up one winter in an art store in Rome. It was bound with an elastic that held together that copy book and the beginnings of a travelogue-cum-spiritual quest book, roughed out on some thirty pages of typing paper, the kind that used to come in one single 200-page sheaf connected by perforations, and another ten pages of loose airmail sheets. I'd started writing out what felt like a life changing immersion in Zanskar some eighteen months after my adventure, in the mideighties. I attempted to convert my fragmented notes, scrawled under the stars and by smoky fires, into a book only to abandon my efforts midway through, for a number of reasons that only became clear decades later. For thirty-seven years those pages moved with me. They came to every rented house and collective living experiment, every apartment in a handful of European countries, to the East Coast and the West Coast and East again, through every happy time and every period of dark despair. I kept that yellow folder through everything, not knowing why; it just was always important in some indeterminant way. Whatever the reason, I was never tempted to part with it. I always felt this journal had a story to tell.

It's time for that story now.

My wish is that you feel touched and inspired on your own journey. That you feel validated in your musings and struggles to find your way. That, above all, you feel the wings of your heart and the gusts of freedom raise you up.

    I believe that's why I carried that folder all these years and why now, in these uncertain and tumultuous times, this story decided it wants to be told.

Amy Edelstein
Philadelphia, January 2021
Zanskar, July 1983

Having developed enthusiasm to awaken,
I will place my mind in concentration;
For the person whose mind is distracted
lives between the fangs of disturbing thoughts.

Through solitude of the body and mind
no distractions will occur;
Therefore, I will forsake the worldly life
and discard all distorted conceptions.

SHANTIDEVA
(7TH – 8TH CENTURY)

Chapter One
Crossing the Threshold

The road from Srinagar to Kargil was treacherous at best. The buses were old and crowded way beyond capacity. The way had just been opened to traffic after a particularly severe winter and many sections of the road had been washed away. In Dras, known as one of the coldest inhabited spots on earth, the road was flanked by snow walls fifteen feet high. The Indo-Tibetan border guard had cut through the snow field to allow for limited transit. The springtime sun worked to erode the ice blockade while underneath the ice deposits coursed a river over a foot deep.

It was the end of June, later in the year than was usual for the thaw, and villagers accustomed to receiving supplies in May were anxious to replenish their stocks. Not long ago, the Srinagar-Leh road had been only a caravan trail, but a dependency on mass-produced goods had since been established. In 1983, Leh itself had become a major tourist attraction in northern India, drawing some 15,000 tourists during its short two-month season. Kashmiri merchants who had expanded into the Tibetan market worried about their losses due to the shortened season, as did the Tibetan guest house owners and the cobblers who had come from Delhi and beyond to work the pleasant streets of Leh.

It had taken me what felt like forever to get on this road, hanging out on houseboats in Kashmir with other freaks and travelers, waiting to find someone with the hunger to explore the inner and the outer. Everyone said they were interested, just not now, as they smoked a little more hashish and sloppily strummed Bob Marley tunes. Finally, I just couldn't wait through another round of "No Woman, No Cry" and squeezed my pack into a crowded seat of the thrice-weekly bus that went from Srinagar to Kargil. They didn't like you to bring your pack inside the bus, preferring to tie them all on the roof, but things tended to go missing that way and I couldn't afford to be without any of the small provisions or meager cooking utensils I carried. I was dressed in a dark blue flowered Kashmiri kurta pyjama, thin baggy cotton pants and a tunic that hung to my knees. With a shawl around my head, I could go relatively unnoticed; blending in was the best way to travel as a young woman alone in this part of the world.

"Are you one man or two?" the Indian men liked to ask me. "Ekli," I would answer. Just one, on my own.

The bus trip was exciting because of the destination but fortunately uneventful in actuality. Our driver was careful. More than a few buses had careened around a corner, cutting too close and tumbling hundreds of feet over the edge. The butterflies fluttered through my body as the bus put more distance between me and the honeymoon destination of Dal Lake. The emerald jewel in India's crown, Srinagar was a truly imperial setting with magnificent waters replete with gondolas, regal fir trees, and hospitable Muslim culture. Yet I was anxious to get to the high hills, the scraggly rocks, and barren mountainscapes filled with hidden treasures. I couldn't wait to drink in the textures, minerals, and solitude, and visit the nunneries and monasteries where, for 2,300 years, people had immersed themselves in meditation and other practices to quell the demons of the mind and illuminate the heart with the blinding light of pristine clarity. This was what was pulling me, coupled with the longing to be far from industrialization, away from the roads and buildings, away from the stuff of the modern world. I was heading to Zanskar, where the valley floor was 3,000 meters above sea level, and the mountains and the passes I would cross rose up from there.

I was following a yearning just to walk. Day after day, week after week, walking with a simplicity that stilled the mind, walking through distractions so I could finally see. I wanted to let all the flusters and ripples of my thoughts become smooth like a mirror, revealing my own mind's defilements in bold relief, exposed to be polished down. The seeker's quest is about clear seeing, staying with the journey in the face of the passing parade of harsh or tempting worlds, both inner and outer. The promise of the spiritual path is to burn through delusion and finally reveal the adamantine brilliance of our own innate, enlightened nature.

I wasn't sure if I had the skills for the journey I was embarking on, either the mountaineering or the meditative ones, but I was going anyway. That was always my way, part curious, part feisty, part feminist rebel, overestimating the reliability of my instincts, trusting the protectorship I always felt and, in large part, unaware of the dangers of the way. So I found myself, bouncing on the hard seat of the Indian bus, peering out dust-streaked windows and holding the acupressure points three fingerwidths in on my wrists to alleviate my road sickness. The snow-grey sky stretched above as I headed towards the oldest Buddhist valley in the world.

Zanskar sits at the very northernmost tip of India, on the westernmost edge of the Tibetan Plateau. It is nestled right between Pakistan and China, just underneath Afghanistan and Tajikistan, and up until contemporary times, 2019, had been part of the predominantly Muslim state of Kashmir. It is remote and prime for geo-political power struggles. The Indian government had only opened region to tourists in 1976, and travelers were still few and far between.

All this was far from my mind as I pulled out my Indian Army map with the rough outlines of the mountains and their elevations in concentric, kidney-shaped ovals. It might as well have been a jewel-studded guide to a treasure of inestimable value, for I was studying it go on a great journey and seek enlightenment. The map was marked with lines for rivers, dashed lines for footpaths, carets for mountain passes. I estimated that the journey from Kargil to Padum and back north again towards Leh, some 500 kilometers, up and down and up and down, again and again, through some of the highest mountains in the region, would take four to six weeks. It was early summer but all across the range it had been a long spring and snow was still heavy in the mountains. My heart fluttered like being in love, a little happy, a little light-headed, and a little afraid.

Driving most of the day, we arrived in Kargil, a Shiite Muslim town, not my final destination but our stop for the night. I stretched my legs and jostled off the bus. I looked around, breathing it all in. When you travel for long periods of time, you develop a new kind of eye, one that sees the surface and also takes in the rhythm of a place. Where is it safe? Where is it questionable? Where do the locals shop and eat? What colors and styles are the local dress and how do they move, eat, gesture? I loved this part of arriving in a new place. Meeting my surroundings with all of my senses, we got to know each other. I looked around in Kargil, picking out the *dhaba* where I'd have a meal and the dormitory where I'd stay the night. It was dirty, no doubt about it. This was a night to put my plastic rain poncho on top of a most likely bed bug-ridden mattress.

The atmosphere was much like a truck stop in any part of the world, grimy and unwelcoming. No women were on the streets. Walls were thickly adorned with posters of the Ayatollah Khomeini. The next morning, men came out early to trade and a few small boys played in the rancid gutters. I bought some simple provisions: dried soy nuggets, which were light to carry and good protein; more matches and candles, essential to get cooking fires lit; and a few extra batteries for my torch. It was Ramadan and impossible to find cooked food before sundown. I was told that the girls in the town began to fast when they were nine years old while boys began the observance at fifteen. It seemed fitting to their customs; the girls began their hard labor early, their sacrifices were exacting throughout their life.

As I wandered through the backstreets, I came across a small garden with a view of the slate-grey river. Only half surprised to see familiar faces, I spotted two friends from Dharamsala sitting having tea. On the road, I had come to know that familiar faces might appear in the most unlikely places, and reappear months or years and countries later. I joined them for hot chai and company. These two had also hoped to explore the remote and enticing Zanskar valley. They had not been able to get bus tickets in Srinagar and decided to hitchhike, ignoring Indian restrictions against riding in lorries. Their truck had overturned on the way, one of the many metal carcasses that our bus had passed. An older

Indian man had suffered fatal wounds and my American friend had broken several ribs. Fortunately, her husband sustained only minor bruises and was able to care for her these last two weeks. After the accident, they were transported to a small one-room clinic in Kargil with no electricity or running water. They said the "doctor" had one needle and one type of injection to relieve pain, which he administered indiscriminately, and the room was infested with cockroaches, lice, and rats.

Still, they were in good spirits despite the near tragedy. She was most disturbed because she was unable to sit for her morning meditation practice. They had recently taken initiations from the warm and delightful Lama Yeshe at Tushita Monastery and had long prayer commitments that they were required to recite each day. She tried to smile despite her bruised torso and confided in me that Lama Yeshe had warned her of a threat to her life before she'd left. He'd prescribed special pujas and mantras for her to fulfill to ward off the danger. She had dutifully carried out all but one of the instructions; she had not saved an animal's life. Tibetans believe that if one saves an animal from death, for example, buying a chicken or goat from the butcher and setting it free, one acquires great merit which has the power to ward off threats to one's person. She felt sure her injury could have been prevented had she followed all the Lama's instructions.

I left them, comforted to have found other familiar faces in such a forbidding village but also a bit nervous. Had I really prepared myself for the dangers I might meet? Was I ready to accept the consequences? Was I willing to face and walk through my fears? Could a woman alone cross the great snowy peaks I saw in the distance? I didn't have answers, only background worries. Having made it this close, I knew I was going to go on. I trusted that all would be well. My heart lifted. The valley was drawing me in. There was no need to articulate all the reasons, circumstances, or karmic propensities leading up to my entry into one of the highest valleys of the world; I simply knew that I was going.

When the bus left the next morning for the Suru stop, which was not really a town but more of an indentation in the road not much larger than a wide shoulder, the Muslim passengers chanted loudly for the protection of Allah. It was a custom to bring protection to the journey, and I felt it was a welcome request for this one. The road was bumpy, more like the promise of a road than an actuality, the smoothing and chipping down of the rocks had yet to happen. The Zanskari men smiled, carefree, with fragrant yellow roses stuck jauntily behind their ears or between their teeth.

In Sankyo, we passed women with kind faces dressed all in black, plucking weeds and *subji* from the wheatfields. Their light skin and almond eyes made it obvious they were of a different tribe than the people of Kargil and their noses, unpierced, seemed strangely un-Indian. They were strikingly beautiful yet isolated in their world separated from men. I smiled at them through the dusty window. They spoke Balti there, a kind of Tibetan language written in a Perso-Arabic script. I had taught myself to read Arabic script haltingly, so I could make out the bus signs in Kashmir. I doubted I would see much of any road signs here, written in any language. Now that we'd left the teeny metropolis of Kargil, all of one block of shops and a few handfuls of stone houses, the only writing I expected to see were Tibetan texts in the monasteries. The language was also going to be an interesting mix; I figured I'd piece together my Hindi, Urdu, a few words in Tibetan, and whatever else I could muster or pull out of thin air. I'd come to find that while travelling I could access a sort of universal language. Whether in Pokhara, Uttar Kashi, or Manali, in the mountain villages, there was a way of communicating which opened up the door to so much kindness, welcome, and generosity.

The clouds cleared as I jumped off the bus and looked at the rocky road for the last time. I had arrived at the entrance of the valley. Without ceremony or really a marker of any kind, I was to begin. I looked around me. It seemed my journey had already begun. I thought I'd have some flatland to stretch my legs and warm up but there was very little lead before I started to climb. The trail wound straight up the hill that rose in front of me. I didn't remember seeing it, it wasn't drawn on my map, if it wasn't so definitive and solid and high I would have rubbed my eyes to dispel the vision. A mist had settled in the vee of the valley and there was a chill in the air. I looked around, no one but me, the bus and all its riders now dissolved in the distance.

I pulled the crystal-sharp air into my lungs, looked

around again, and aloneness gave way to freedom. Challenge and freedom. The skin on my cheeks tingled with the call of the unknown, the commitment to deepen, the determination to follow through. Even though I wasn't sure how to articulate my ultimate goal, at least I knew my immediate goal, which was up, up, up and beyond the chortens I could see at the top of the ridge. Chortens are the lighthouses of the mountain ranges. Squat stone pillars a few feet high, they are built to mark the spot where it is possible to cross the mountain ridge. Their shape and their white flags guide the traveler to safe passage, east or west of danger or impassable rock faces and glacial walls.

Just beyond the pass peeked the promise of Nun and Kun, two massive mountains, and the somber entrance of Zanskar, the Copper Valley. I had been told the hamlet of Pakarchik, some twenty houses or so, was near enough to reach that afternoon. The stream to my right was bedecked with long lavender irises. Fat marmots, sleek curious fellows, rose on their rear legs to survey this odd-looking traveler. Two golden eagles circled around the valley in easy grace. Auspicious.

Climbing over moss and clay-colored mud, the tip of the ridge seemed within reach, but the path kept unfolding vertically. I never seemed to get nearer to the top and the chorten disappeared out of sight behind a fold in the rock. At one point I stood still, surveying the surroundings, unsure if I was really on a path. I had hurried ahead, not careful to check the way, thinking I would know. Now I found myself confronted with the actuality that I really wasn't sure of quite a lot of things. As for the path I was trying to find, there were so many little trails hardened by the hooves of various animals, domesticated and wild alike, it was hard to say which one was the path. The light was taking a turn towards evening. I had a little time but not much. Clouds blanketed the sky. Nothing but scrub and shale lay in sight, the stream now far below me and to the east. I smelled dusk in the air, the muskiness of evening.

I wasn't going to make it to the top of the ridge and down the other side as I'd thought. But that was all right. I'd been walking for five hours and I had no real need to be anywhere or reach any destination. Everything was open. I looked around and found a place to spend my first night. Stowing my pack in a niche, I spread my sleeping gear between two rocks, thermal pad, sleeping bag, covered with a plastic rain poncho to keep out the condensation. I gathered some handfuls of dry twigs from the base of a few dwarfed bushes, pleased to find bits of wood where there seemed to be none so far above the treeline. Moving quickly, unsure when darkness would overtake me, I rationed out water for tea and dahl. I had no appetite at this elevation and my head was pounding but I knew I should eat. A light drizzle began. The air was misty, slate-colored. To the west, the sky stretched on and on. When I finally lay down, my feet stretched over the edge. I felt happy to be able to fend for myself in the lap of the mountain, moving at my own pace. I was fed and secure on the side of a cliff. Night fell and held me near. In the mountains, the darkness seems even closer than close, different than when I would feel the night outside my window. The sky stretches back to infinity, and the countless jeweled stars glitter, flickering, speaking to one another in some language I could not divine. There are conversations occurring at a level of the cosmos that we are just too small to hear.

I woke a few times but saw no moon or stars to help me guess the time of night. It was so deeply still and vast. I felt both secure and exposed, a fragile form laid bare on the heights. It was cold, but not too cold; the cloud cover kept me warm. When I did doze, I felt I was dreaming not my own dreams, but some song of the universe that I was hearing snippets of in my sleep. The melody penetrated layers of my consciousness, like those plaintive fragments of whale song, long verses that convey history and secrets and hold the key to greater harmony, if we could only truly hear. I felt stories were being told to me that I couldn't yet decipher, still I heard them, code and all, and their parables were etched into my sleeping mind. Dreamtime came and went, and with it my first night in the Zanskari valley passed.

Those who have obtained a human life, rich in virtues,
by collecting merit over innumerable eons,
who then, due to confusion,
fail to accumulate even the slightest merit
Are like explorers
who go to a land covered with jewels
And return home empty-handed.

ARYASURA
(4TH CENTURY CE)

Chapter Two
Precious Human Birth

In the morning, after the sun had been up for an hour or so, a little bit of blue sky opened up and I could see the chortens again at the top of the pass. Morning was more practical, time to pack up and walk. The pass seemed straight above me. Not yet acclimatized to the altitude or the rigor, it took all my effort and willpower to continue the slow way, picking out one foothold at a time. I felt sure there must have been an easier path somewhere, and I was instead following the one meant for sure-footed mountain goats, not a lead-footed Western woman. My body quivered when the glacial wind picked up and pierced through my wool *faran*. Nun Kun's glacier gleamed blue to my right. Chortens dotted the way like stone trolls merrily squatting by the path.

Suddenly, instead of being far from the crest, I was there. At the top. I had made it! Even though I was breathing hard, now here, the pass didn't seem quite so high. Height is relative, especially when you are in the shadow of such majestic peaks. To my right, in the East, Nun and Kun stretched further upward. They were awe-inspiring. I felt prayerful and stilled by the wonder of it all. Gasping from the elevation and the bitter wind in my face, I drank my fill of Nun rising 7,135 meters, Kun at 7,077 meters, and the massive jumbled Shatat glacier snaking between them. The glacier breathed in and out, walls of turquoise ice higher than

I could gauge with my eyes, and always shifting. At its mouth, it spewed out rough pewter-colored water, a river wide, churning, and life-forbidding. The mountains emanated a presence and a message. I wasn't yet wise enough to sense what it was, but I felt it. I heard it somewhere in my being, took it in, and gave respect and thanks to the forces so much greater and older than I.

The presence of the high mountains kept me moving. As still and solitary as the landscape was, the range had its own life and it pushed me forward, propelling me to take my next step. It was another language for the practices I learned from the Vedanta teachings I'd studied for months in Rishikesh and Varanassi, and the Buddhist teachings I'd been learning everywhere I could from books, from Theravadans, from Tibetan masters: keep practicing, keep purifying, keep ascending to realize God or Awakened Mind. You never know exactly how far you are. Always work to generate more merit. Dedicate it to the alleviation of suffering of the countless sentient beings in all the different realms. Once you commit and take the *bodhisattva* path to heart, as content as you can be in the moment, with everything utterly full and utterly empty, perfect as it is, there is always more compassion to realize, ever more wisdom and harmony to bring into the world, more heaven to bring to earth. Enlightenment, as huge a goal as it is, is still not the end point. A bodhisattva never rests, postponing their own liberation until all beings have been awakened too. And yet they lack nothing, strive for nothing, and wait for nothing else to happen to be fully happy, fully at rest, fully being. Here in the high mountains, paradox, patience, transference of consciousness from lifetime to lifetime felt alive, tangible not remote or abstract.

Just before leaving for my adventure in the mountains, I had been invited to take the Refuge Vows. I'd declined. It was a lifelong commitment, I needed to think about it more. I wasn't interested in wrapping myself in the cloak of another custom, culture, and set of conditions for my own awakening. I also knew that if I committed, I had to really mean it, and even though I was already compelled by the call of Spirit, it was going to take me some time to steep in the understanding of a life committed to enlightenment, to see if this was the right choiceless next step. When I finally did take the vows, three years later, it was at once the life I was already living, and a marker that separated my meandering from a more conscious and intentional commitment on the path.

That day is still crisp in my mind. It was early summer 1986. I walked down the forested path in Dharamsala, from Tushita Retreat Center to a very small makeshift refugee house in McLeod Ganj. Tucked in between many other one room houses was a simple structure, pieced together with flattened out cans of cooking oil, mud stucco, jaunty red and orange begonias in empty milk powder cans lining the walkway. Lama Zopa Rinpoche, then young, and the young head of the Foundation for the Preservation of the Mahayana Tradition, successor to the ebullient Lama Yeshe, was our translator. Four westerners, including myself made our way into the meditation retreat and home of Kirti Tsenshab Rinpoche, one of the Dalai Lama's revered Senior Tutors. We barely fit, and left the door open to make room for the spill over.

Kirti TsenshabLa was known to be one of the most knowledgeable and erudite scholars of the Gelugpa tradition. I expected him to be dry and somewhat intimidating but when I saw him, my nervousness melted and I was taken into his field of joy. His smile was far bigger than his thin, wrinkled, and worn face. His eyes twinkled behind his glasses, and his warmth felt like the closest embrace from the infinite arms of the cosmos. I stood right before him as he sat, cross legged, wrapped in maroon robes.

He asked me some questions, Lama Zopa translating, "Was I ready to take refuge?" Meaning, was I ready to dedicate my life to pursuing what was true and wholesome and to discarding ignorant and negative states of mind for the sake of all beings? I checked my heart. For me prayer was not something I did to someone or for something, prayer was reading the book of my truest intentions. Especially at this moment, I wanted to be sure of the words of my soul, clear and unflinching, regardless of what it might be and where it might lead. Yes, I was sure. I also knew that the path I was following was not a Buddhist, Jewish, or any other tradition that bound me to one thing and not to another. My commitment was to follow truth, that pathless land. I was committing with all my heart and soul to the principles of the vows I was about to take, principles I already had embraced. Sure of my intention, I looked into the great teacher's eyes, repeated the refuge vows one by one, bowing each time, my black chuba meeting the clean dirt floor.

"I take refuge in the possibility and examples of the awakened ones. I take refuge in the teachings that separate delusion from clarity. I take refuge in the community of practitioners, who, throughout the ages, support one another to realize liberation from fear, greed, and ignorance for the benefit of all beings."

But as I was entering the mouth of the Zanskar Valley, the bright beginning of summer in June 1983, the decision to commit to the bodhisattva path, as it was laid out by the adepts, was still coalescing in me. I had always been propelled by a desire to realize truth but I needed to see what a life lived unselfconsciously and unapologetically to those ideals could mean. I was still a novice on the path, even though at times it felt like there were old wisps of memories of lifetimes of practice inside my young body.

Now I was setting out on an adventure that, as challenging as the outer journey would likely be, I knew the hardest part was going to be its inner one. I was committed. And I was scared. Walking on my own, I had time to mull over with some of the questions and paradoxes of the teachings I had recently been privileged to hear. One of the ones that intrigued me most was the Buddhist belief that we all already have Buddha nature. Rather than a Judeo-Christian view of original sin or needing to build a fence of rules to keep from transgressing the most essential spiritual laws, this way of seeing gave everyone inherent confidence in themselves. It's part of the reason why Tibetans seem so happy and secure in spite of living simple lives or even living in the shadow of recent horrific violence against their homeland, their people, and their religion. This teaching is that our nature is of fundamental goodness, our essence is inherent wholeness and awakened consciousness. But our own Buddha-nature remains more or less in potential while we work to evolve our own consciousness, clarify our understanding, and purify our intentions and motivations. Awakening, our individual evolution, is an unfolding where we return home where we've never left. Like in a dream, we pass through our lives mostly unconscious, unaware of who we really are. That essential nature has been obscured by the momentum of our negative karma, the accumulated effects of our unskillful and harmful actions, which hides what's there like storm clouds hide the sun. Even once realized, the seeker, now become a finder, still keeps on their journey, living out their lives in service, renouncing their final release from this world of birth and death until every single sentient being in all the realms are liberated, freed from the bondage of suffering, delusion, and perpetual cyclic existence. The realized have infinite time to uplift others, for immersion in meditation erases all but the limitless present. We need that dimension of the infinite because there is precious little time in our short and finite precious human birth.

The Tibetans say the best birth is the human one. It's the Goldilocks principle, not too much, not too little, just right. We have enough suffering to propel us on the path, but not too much to mire us in impossible pain. We have enough good fortune to be able to come in contact with the dharma but not too much good fortune to get lost among the pleasures of the god-realms. We have enough free will to become dedicated, motivated, and vigilant and enough discipline to tame the wild monkeys of our minds. They say you must practice with every breath, always reciting mantras, always cultivating *bodhicitta* or great compassion for others, because the human birth is over in an instant when measured against the time it takes to evolve towards Buddhahood.

My aspiration to live this precious human birth well kept me going, but with my healthy dose of postmodern self-doubt, mostly I felt I wasn't ever doing enough, wasn't doing it right, wasn't giving as much as I needed to, and whatever I realized was never going to be what it should. My Eastern teachers told me this troubled state of mind was common among Western practitioners. They had had to get used to it because in the East, most renunciates wrestle with overblown pride and confidence in themselves rather than this kind of crippling doubt. The teachings were bending to accommodate the Western mind, I wondered what they might be losing.

Regardless, there I was, heading into the valley to walk my way into a more awakened condition. In spite of my overly complicated mind, I was committed, as awake as I could be, eyes-open and ready to learn. Walking in the high mountains for me paralleled the wheel of becoming, illustrating the repetitive cycle of the restless human birth. Time and distance stretched endlessly, an infinite present, a single flow. At the same time, each cycle of a day, like each human life, felt far too short. I could see how easy it was to walk from morning to night with the same level of response to desire, fear, and ignorance. No growth, no insight. I imagined it might also become easy, with practice, to walk through each day shattering small shackles of delusion and breaking free from the tangle of unskillful, karma-creating activity. That's what I was here to find out.

My second night came quickly, hurrying me along. I had climbed up and over the other side of the ridge. It had been a long and full day. I was starting to see that time moved differently here. I found a little indent in the rock. Not much of a cave but warmer than being out in the open. Half a year earlier, I had sold my tent in Kathmandu, to another traveler outside in a little shop in Thamel, the secondhand trekkers area. It was too heavy to carry, too bulky for the buses, and if the locals could weather the elements without a one, I would learn to as well. I was pleased to be out of the wind, at least for now, and set up to spend my second night under a perfect overhang facing the river, secluded and protected from the elements with plenty of wood nearby. I sipped Kashmiri tea, a mixture of black tea, cardamom, and cinnamon, and rested as the rice steamed. The warm food was simple and good. I snuggled in for the night and fell into a deep dreamless sleep.

The roar of an avalanche startled me awake. Afraid that it was above me, I stepped out of the cave to see thick mist steaming off the river and clouds chasing each other across the night sky. Boulders had tumbled into the water, the endless change of what seemed so solid and so permanent. Life was precious. Life was good.

The next morning, I packed up quickly and was off with the first light. Sometimes a thick chute of snow snaked down the mountainside, dropping off at the river. From a distance, it looked like a knife-spread of icing, but it could be more than twenty feet deep and treacherous to cross.

I crossed a number of smaller ones, which made my heart pump wildly and my palms sweat. They scared me. Without an ice axe, if I slipped I would continue to slide until dropped, unceremoniously, into the river. I kept my eyes glued to the ground and moved in slow motion, at one with the movement of my feet and their contact with the earth. My vision focused in so I was aware of all the small muscles that made each step forward. Fear kept me alert. The concentration brought a clarity of mind, a combination of expansiveness and laser-sharp attention. I passed two snow bridges that spread across the wild khaki water. I had never imagined such perfect engineering feats. Huge, more than fifty meters across, yet from this distance they seemed so fragile, arced so delicately beside the chunky glacial mouth. One massive bridge collapsed right before my eyes, icebergs rocking in the current. I shuddered with the immediacy of being alive, and the impermanence I'd just witnessed. Nothing lives forever. Not the largest mountains, not the glaciers, not any single life.

Nun and Kun moved out of my view as I curved around a village of about fifteen houses and stumbled onto the rough army road that had been built just a few years earlier. It was far easier to follow than the small tracks that spiderwebbed up and down the scree-covered face of the hill. The road followed the Suru river, and for much of the next few days, I would follow it too. The locals called it the Karcha Nar. The road was not much of one, snow and avalanche debris obscured the way and dozens of spring streams, several inches deep and often several yards wide, crossed its surface.

What will you do with your one precious human birth? The lama asked on a ten-day retreat I'd just finished. How far will you go in this lifetime? Will you reach the yonder shore? Even as dull and lost in materialism or grasping as human beings are, human birth is said to be so rare. How rare? He told us the story. Imagine, the Buddha taught, that the whole world was covered with water. In that vast sea floated a single wooden yoke. The wind would blow it east and then another wind would blow it west. It bobbed up and down on the surface of the vast ocean. Now, how rare would it be if a single one-eyed sea tortoise rose out of the ocean in random places, once every one-hundred years, and happened to put his head right through that small wooden yoke? Taking a human birth, the Buddha taught, is even more rare than that. Was I doing enough in my precious human birth? Was I developing discrimination and altruism? My way was leading me through the mountains, and my heart was singing to be there with their presence. Was it enough? It felt like all I could do now. The rest would have to unfold.

I passed a few tiny villages along the river. In one, a young man named Mohammed invited me in for chai and thick round flatbreads. There were two women in the fields who came into the house when they saw us. They were quiet and somewhat withdrawn. They were not Zanskaris but Dards, descendants of a 5,000-year-old Indo-Aryan culture, some said to be ancestors of Alexander the Great's army when they moved into this region some 2,000 years ago. With roots in shamanic practices, many Dards have now also embraced Islam or Buddhism, or a combination of both, weaving it all into their tightly knit small community. They have penetrating clear eyes that seemed to look right through me and beyond to some earlier time I couldn't see. Mohammed told me he was twenty-one and married but he wasn't happy with his wife. He said, to my surprise, "My religion is no good for women." Then, by way of explanation, told me the story of the other woman who was living with them. She had left her husband, who was no good. She was only twenty, no children, and now had a life alone ahead of her. She was not allowed to remarry in their custom and was considered used and disgraced. Life can be so hard.

I thanked them for their hospitality and kindness and moved on. My journey had just begun and I wanted to keep moving. On the way, I passed a monk from Ringdom Gompa traveling with two friends, then later I crossed several Tibetans with horses on the path, and finally one black-clad Muslim woman with a huge load of wood on her back. I eventually found myself walking on a partial road, mostly washed out, with snow and rocks covering the way. Small brown rabbits twitched their noses when they smelled me and I could hear the birds twittering though they were hard to spot, camouflaged or hidden in the pussy willows and reeds along the rivulets. The rock litter quickly grew more dense. It became easier to walk on the small path, as the animals had trodden the way smooth. While it was easier to walk on it was also easier to take a wrong turn. The horses and yaks roamed all over to graze. I had a direction I was trying to head in. I repeatedly had to switchback and retrace my steps, making my progress slow but measurable. The higher I went, the heavier my pack became. In the next village, I promised myself, I would lighten it up. Two books are hardly essential. Three shirts are two too many.

Those who unhesitatingly embrace and tenderly serve
All suffering creatures during this degenerate age,
Just as a loving mother painstakingly cares
For even the most wayward of her children,
They alone are the teachers of the holy life
Who authentically walk the Buddha Way.

JETSUN JE TSONGKHAPA
(1357-1419)

Chapter Three
Initiation Takes Many Forms

The way became more sandy and smooth, unlike the litter of rocks of the first few days. The chasm widened into a green pasture crisscrossed with many small rivulets. My stomach was, unfortunately, beginning to churn. Delhi belly, or rather Kargil belly, was a queasy, sour squishing that comes when the amoebas or microbes that grow in dirty cooking pots, cleaned with even dirtier ever-damp rags, take up residence in the intestines. By late afternoon, I was tired. The road curved around a bend and tucked itself neatly under a rocky overhang, revealing a well-used cave. With walls and ceiling blackened from the campfires of other travelers, old char in the firepit, and a musty smell, it seemed welcoming enough and I crawled in. Not the most beautiful accommodations and not the most uplifting view, but rest was necessary. I cramped and curled into myself all night, feeling the flush of fever and the chill of sweat run through my bones. Physically, it was miserable, but the sheer exhilaration of being here, on this adventure, carried me through.

When the weak light of the morning seeped in, I weighed my options. I could keep moving forward in hopes of walking it off or rest for a few days so that whatever I ate would pass through and not lodge in my system. The cave was so unappealing, I decided to move on. Hoisting my pack onto my back, it felt ten pounds heavier than the day before. My strength had dissipated. But after the dank cave, the fresh air felt good on my face, clean and healthy. I drank it in and took slow, even steps, relieved to see a long, flat expanse stretch ahead of me. The narrow valley floor was covered with brilliant green. Chubby marmots surveyed the scene, whistling and pontificating to any and all who would listen. Snow clouds covered the sky from above, a blanket I could all but pull and tuck under the valley's chin.

I'd been walking for a few hours and was ready for a rest when I saw a Tibetan man squatting by the river in the distance, filling his chai pot with water. I trained my eyes just past him and made out the tent of his party. He wore a white wool jacket, Ladakhi style, crossed in front of his body with extra-long arms. I couldn't tell if they were traders, villagers, or maybe even a party of monks with a guide. I walked a little further and was soon in front of their camp.

There were six Tibetan men comfortably set up in the spacious tent, sewn from a Japanese parachute. Though it was only late morning, it felt like midday; walking was slow in the light drizzle. They invited me in, brewed pot after pot of salt-butter tea, and pulled *tsampa*—roast barley flour, a dietary staple—by the handful from large canvas sacks. Sometimes they added a few pieces of bone-dry cheese or some highly carbonated yogurt called *sho*. Mostly they just tossed small handfuls of tsampa flour, dry, into their mouths. When I tried to imitate them, I got it all over my face and began to sneeze and cough. They laughed. Being with them was easy, no hurry, no worry, an invisible web of happiness wove a tapestry in the space between them. They each seemed to hold different stations, at the same time there was an easy equality. Unlike near a Hindu's cooking fire, there was no hierarchy around the pot. They all dished out the tea brew with two small hand-hammered copper ladles and two of the younger men toasted perfect *chapatis* on a piece of scrap metal which most likely came from an airplane's wreckage. I noticed that their boiling pots were higher above the coals than I had placed mine and that they only used one or two sticks in their fire at a time. I'd been having a hard time getting my water to boil. Their trick seemed to be creating more heat with a little distance from the fire. So much to learn!

Stuffed with the breakfast they gave me and with the excuse of rain clouds appearing, I asked them if I could lie down for a mid-morning nap. It was relaxing and peaceful being around them. Something deep was pulling my eyelids down and my mind into sleep. Two men brought some thick Tibetan carpets to soften the ground. I leaned back onto my rolled-up thermal mat. Already almost asleep, I was vaguely aware of them covering me with a coarse yak-hair blanket. I felt so welcomed, not fussed over but cared for and safe, even in a group of six strange men. The air was free of suspicion, tension, or any sense of harm. They were alert, guileless but not naive, generous but not condescending. It was an unfamiliar feeling that made me more at home than I had almost ever felt. They all seemed so at ease with themselves and each other, actually happy.

This feeling is Zanskar. That quality of home. People lighthearted, content, at peace. No friction, no competition. Sure, everyone is human and has their own preferences and edges. But whether it's the harsh environment, or the spaciousness and small population, or the sense of all being dependent on one another in the high mountains, or the living spiritual teachings of impermanence and the universality of the human experience, or their constant work taming negative states of mind, or their belief in our inherent Buddha nature, or their commitment to cultivate infinite compassion, or every one of those elements mixed with some magic secret sauce, Zanskaris are deeply happy. Being with them immersed me in a way of being so unfamiliar it made my heart catch. So kindhearted. A different kind of love. Watching them, made real how people can simply be with each other and how that ease brings joy. I would experience these qualities over and over again among the Zanskaris as I was welcomed into their homes. In this gathering, whatever I was feeling was even more so.

When I awoke, it was late afternoon. The bank of clouds had cleared to the east and the sky invited a stroll into the loveliness. Finding my land legs again after the hard night, I walked a ways up the river to wash, smelling the spring grasses and little yellow flowers. There were little bits of clouds to the west, letting through shafts of late afternoon light and painting golden streaks across the mountainside in the distance. That part of the valley ran almost directly east to west. The sun traveled along the backbone of the sky's blue ribbon, a bright band that lay between the black silhouettes of the mountains. The river wiggled its way into the distance. It was a magical valley and the moment was kind.

When I returned to the tent, the eldest in the group, a Lama, so marked by his distinctive maroon hat and the reverence the others showed him, had brought out sacred Tibetan texts wrapped in yellow cloth. The scriptures the Tibetans use are a narrow, rectangular shape and unbound; sheaf after sheaf of block-printed verses are sandwiched between two pieces of wood. I wondered how they could put them back in order if the wind ever scattered the pages. The Lama handed each of the others some pages and they chanted for a while. Afterwards, they took out their wooden malas and recited mantras. The Rinpoche wore primitive eyeglasses, a sign of his importance I guessed, and had a jolly if somewhat removed nature. They told me he was over old, maybe even over one-hundred years old. His knobby hands could easily have seen that many years, but his voice was strong and his body agile. He had been sent to a monastery to study when he was a child and was steeped in the gentleness and wisdom of his education and his practice.

The man who spoke the best Hindi and a little English told me they were returning from visiting several of the large monasteries in the valley. He pointed to the elderly lama with his rakish hat, "He was just in L.A. He travels all over the world."

I assumed it was my poor Hindi and that I just didn't understand him. But a few years later, while studying at Deer Park Buddhist Center in Madison, Wisconsin, I showed the other students a few photographs.

"Oh! That's Lama so-and-so!" One excitedly said when he saw the Rinpoche in the tent and instinctively touched his forehead with hands folded in prayer. "He's a very high lama. I saw him once, years ago in L.A."

We talked back and forth as much as possible in broken Hindi and Urdu since my Tibetan was still so minimal. I tried to tell them about my illness. I was weak from my fever and dysentery the night before and had been suffering from a recurring knot in my shoulder.

"You are in luck," the attendant told me. "Rinpoche is not only a great master, he is also a great doctor, a Tibetan doctor. Let him look."

When the Lama finished the puja, his attendant spoke a few words to him, and he reached over for his bag and pulled out a medicine kit. This was not the kind of ordinary medicine kit with stethoscope and blood pressure cuff, it held vials with pills in various shades of brown, red, green, and black, and other herbs and ground minerals. He took my right wrist in his dry hand. His grip was firm, knowledgeable, and indescribably kind. I felt my whole system relax, one big sigh through my vagal nerve and my facial net. Tibetan medicine starts with taking pulses from both hands. He placed his three fingers on my inner wrist, his fingers were papery and rested lightly but firmly. He looked into the distance then switched hands. When he finished, he started murmuring prayers and closed his eyes. He continued this way for some time. Then he opened his eyes and reached into the many folds of his satchel, pulling out small pouches tied with colored string hanging with little tags. He carried about forty different mixtures with him and the attendant told me he could cure anything from depression to wild animal bites. Lama opened one and took out three dark brown spheres the size of small grapes.

"La," he said.

"Take these," the younger man translated into Hindi. "Chew with hot water. You will feel better tomorrow."

In Tibetan medicine, they first treat the spiritual, the disturbance of the winds or *lungs*, before the physical. It is the opposite of allopathic medicine where we treat the physical first. Tibetans see spiritual disturbances, which result in physical imbalances or illnesses, as something we can more easily address; we have the ability to take action to dispel our ignorance or remedy spiritual imbalances. They see the spiritual level as the least invasive, which is why they start there. Clearing up our own delusion is within our power and therefore the most direct way to cure ourselves and come back into balance or health. It is much harder to fix the physical imbalance, since helping cells regenerate is generally out of reach of our intention, prayer, or mind. Working on the physical level requires some kind of invasive treatment, something external brought inside, whether ingesting of medicinal herbal compounds or binding wounds and fractures.

Tibetans also see illness and injury as karma ripening, as the result of past actions where we caused harm and are now experiencing the inevitable consequences or repercussions. We can avert ongoing difficulty by doing actions that bring merit. These would be acts motivated by compassion, generosity, and our own inquiry into the deeper nature of reality. Illness or injury is not to be complained about, it is to be accepted as the result of our own doing. It can even be of benefit. Karmic ripenings allow us to resolve negative karmic momentum and so continue to evolve to higher and higher levels of wisdom. Even serious illnesses can be seen as averting worse consequences and so are faced directly, with courage, intention, and motivation to develop. With that non-victimized approach, Tibetan medicine becomes a powerful vehicle to transform illness, suffering, fear, regret, and resentment and develop steadiness, strength, self-reliance, compassion, motivation, and even joy. Joy at proceeding on the path, joy at the possibility of perfection, joy at the attainment of Buddhahood in this lifetime, and joy from caring for the benefit of all beings in the realms that we can see and those that are invisible to us. Our own life and our progression on the path to awakening is never seen outside the context of everyone else's wellbeing. It's a powerful cosmology. I had a lot to consider and re-orient in my own attitudes and reactions.

I did as I was told and chewed the brown globules, hopeful. Tibetan pills are large and awful tasting mixtures. They react with the saliva as well as with stomach acids and they must be chewed thoroughly with hot water before swallowing. The Tibetan medicine I had taken in Dharamsala had never done much for my dysentery when I'd taken it then, but this dose seemed to come with an added blessing and so I dutifully chewed.

Even though I was sick, I still felt held and cared for in these wild mountains. The tensions and doubt that I had carried with me ever since I was a child had receded. I felt safe, protected, and loved in a removed, yet very immediate and gentle way. What were the odds of a doctor appearing in the middle of nowhere, tending to me physically and spiritually in a little cocoon of safety and healing, and enveloping me in a field of blessing?

Yet, as immersed as I was in the blessings, for the most part, I think the auspiciousness of the moment escaped my conscious mind. My rational thoughts were so filled with habitual and reductionistic judgments, my many years of training in a deconstructionist postmodern culture. I doubted what the attendant was saying because it didn't make sense to me. L.A.? Europe? Big teacher? Blessings to cure stomach bugs? The other men doted over me and smiled kindly, like an adult over a child who does not grasp the significance of the events transpiring. Neither of us had the language skills to communicate that well and I did not yet have the openness of mind yet to trust what I was already experiencing. The Lama smiled patiently. He seemed to know what was going on in my mind and continued with more prayers and blessings, some from the blue medicine Buddha, others planting the seeds of teachings to ripen at the proper time.

It was my first introduction to the seamlessness of the nomadic ways of life and the powerful monastic tradition. There is an ease and an embeddedness of Buddhist practice in Tibetan culture. It is shared by everyone, and it's part of the conversation and currency of relationships in an unselfconscious way. Practice and responding to life and each other according to the path of enlightenment is as familiar as navigating daily weather patterns. Respected and revered, religion weaves inseparably through all aspects of life. The valley is so remote it has known so little conflict in its entire history that its spiritual traditions and village networks have remained stable and intact. There is harmony and continuity embedded in this land.

Children grow up aspiring to become monastics, wanting the opportunity to study and learn. Most Zanskari children would tell me, wistfully, "I pray to be allowed to become a monk or a nun." They smile so brightly when they express this. It makes their hearts glad. No fear or guilt around the formal practice, joy crosses their faces just thinking about that possibility. Some children have to stay with the family, work the fields, keep the home, tend the animals, and care for younger siblings and older grandparents. Those children speak with pride of their sister or brother who is in the monastery. The monks are the ones working to uplift everyone, to bring the blessings of the Buddhas down to every sentient being in the valley and beyond. What greater gift is there than that? To practice to become a bodhisattva and help all beings?

These families have followed this rhythm for generations, a thousand years or more, in an unbroken tradition. Every family I met in Zanskar and Ladakh had sent one child to the monastery or nunnery. Every family was part of the fabric of study and development, practice and retreat. Generally, families have no more than four children, but even four mouths are a lot to support through the long, harsh winters. Monastics are supported by the whole community and by disciples of their main lamas from afar with donations of food, animals, and money. The monasteries, many clinging to the cliffside, perched on an isolated crag, often own quite a bit of land, which also helps sustain the practitioners so they can spend hours upon hours chanting prayers that resonate in the various realms and echo off the rock walls. Donations to the monasteries bring great merit to the donors. Generosity is an integral part of the Buddhist practice and parents rest assured that their children will be well cared for. Both monks and nuns learn to read texts, and when they come home for family events or to help with the harvest they pass on their knowledge. The level and prevalence of literacy and subtle philosophical understanding in such a rustic environment startled me.

In my familial culture, it wasn't wisdom but knowledge that was prized. It was an unspoken given that myself and my siblings would go to college. Reason, science, and the history of the material world were revered. Education was prized as the key to wealth and security. It was not, as I grew to appreciate, the key to true happiness, well-being, or purpose.

In the Zanskari tradition, education of the mind is a large part of study, but the emphasis is on an understanding of the nature of the mind in order to cultivate right action. Right action is not an end unto itself, it is the means to penetrating clarity, boundless altruism, sublime joy—freedom. Buddhahood meant more than an enlightened realization, it meant abiding in self-arising joy and the perfection of wisdom and caring for all sentient beings, in all the realms, the ones we can see and the ones we can't see.

In Zanskar, families sent their children to develop as individuals for the sake of the karmic continuum of all beings, and so they live in a field where the groundwater of mantra, study, offerings, and meditation permeate the land and the air. Walking in that valley, the westernmost edge of the highest plateau in the world, I felt the influence. It was working in me, changing me from the inside out. Being here, my whole self felt like it was absorbing the nutrients of liberation teachings through the air I breathed, the water I drank, and the rocks and sky I took in, and the people who showed me what it was to live with the currency of compassion and Love.

In spite of my own thick-headedness, I did appreciate my time in that very unusual gathering. They had fun teaching me Ladakhi and I developed a good list of sentences and vocabulary words in my notebook from our time together. Though I was reluctant to leave, we all had our own agendas, they were heading north, I was walking south. The next morning, I thanked them and departed, continuing my journey under cloudy skies that soon broke into light snow flurries. I was leaving the world I'd known behind. The changing terrain nodded in assent.

If you want to totally free yourself from suffering,
it is important to distinguish what to do from what not to
do since you cannot hope to taste the fruit
of beneficial actions that you have not done,
nor escape the consequences of your own harmful actions.

After death, you will follow the course
traced by your actions, good and bad.
Now that you have a choice between two paths,
one that leads up and one that leads down,
do not act in a way opposed to your deepest wishes.

Practice all possible beneficial actions, even the smallest.
Doesn't the accumulation of little drops
end up filling a large jar?

JETSUN MINGYUR PALDRÖN
(1699-1769)

Chapter Four
A Taste of Home

That day, my shoulder continued to pain so badly that sometimes when I looked down a cry escaped my lips. But I kept plugging along. Surprisingly, it did dissipate, and my belly bug calmed. By afternoon both had disappeared. My trip, begun in some ways as a macho expedition, in only a few days now seemed like recalibrated to this place, pace, and preoccupation with the journey of the soul. I was on my own. Alone there was nothing to prove, nothing to be frightened of. My daily task was simple: head southeast along the valley floor. Everything else flowed out of that and a commitment to evolve. The straightforwardness of the trail upended the self-imposed limitations I was in the habit of setting. It had taken courage to deny my doubts and set out, but those doubtful thoughts had, at least so far, posed the greatest and, in fact, only obstacle. Now, I just needed to take one step after another. Follow the path. Pace myself. Allow inner tensions and unresolved issues from my past to unwind. For the most part, not just in this valley but throughout my short life, my fears were my own projections, not justified reactions to the reality I was experiencing. Isn't it often that way? We create our own monsters then squeal in fright?

As I walked, I appreciated the immediacy. Meditation in motion. The joy of openings, of strengths, and of insight uncovered and always more questions to contemplate, questions about spiritual progress, about the nature of mind, about the continuity of consciousness. The object of my meditation was the majesty and monochrome nature of my surroundings. As I rested my sights on the mountains, sky, and valley, I settled into subtlety. Without big and loud distractions, I became aware of simple and subtle changes. Changes in rock color, striation, elevation, wind pattern. Changes in self. I noticed my body undergoing constant movement and flow, from muscle movements to breath, to strength ebbing and regenerating. My thoughts ticked by in a constant display of the pendulum of impermanence. Swaying one way then back again. Observing change is a foundational practice of calm-abiding and a process of purification through self-awareness. This was the perfect place to practice. My own retreat immersion. My own form of meditation in perpetual motion.

Walking in this high valley was like sitting in a long Vipassana retreat. One of my early teachers, a well-known Western teacher, who first started teaching meditation in the West in the early 1970s, had told me that when meditating you keep observing—with minute attention—thoughts and sensations arising and passing away. You string together moments of mindfulness, one after another, until you have an unbroken chain of enlightened awareness. I wasn't so sure about the cumulative or linear process that he described at the time. Enlightenment seemed to me to be a much more radical leap into an entirely different way of seeing and being, but that moment-to-moment awareness has its own rewards. Vipassana or insight practice produces clarity and calm, within which we can discern wholesome and unwholesome habits of mind, unfounded beliefs, and ungenerous wishes. I realized on this trek, I was going to be spending a lot of time witnessing my own constructs of fear and self-doubt. We all have to work through our own nature or karma.

When Siddhartha Gautama made his final steps to awakening, he abandoned all paths and proscribed forms, and watched. He watched himself walking in the jungle, lifting, moving, and placing each step. He watched his breath going in and out. He watched the way mind created images that faded away. He observed and thought deeply about experience, life, directionality, and process. Finally, he sat down under the Bodhi tree, resting the tips of his fingers on the ground, saying, "As the earth is my witness, I will not move until I have penetrated the true nature of all things." While I didn't believe I was necessarily going to get to the yonder shore this particular journey through the mountains, that was my lodestar and walking and witnessing, seeing through the demons in my mind was my plan. And so I walked.

The Buddhists teach that all is in a process of flow, movement, change, transformation, and trans-configuration, whether that change is occurring at a level we are aware of or not is beside the point. Clinging to anything—be it material possessions or self-sense—is called "wrong view," wrong because it is futile. You cannot hold onto what is impermanent. It will flow through your hands like water. It will dissolve into the ether like snow in the sun. It will pass from this lifetime like clouds cross the sky. We get so worked up about slights we receive, a shortcoming that is made public, or an object we so want to possess, that we trade our long-term happiness, the karmic stability that comes from clear seeing, for the short-term relief of rage, humiliation, or attachment.

It seemed obvious to me now that whether I believed in the karmic momentum going from lifetime to lifetime or not, my actions still set into motion a propensity towards goodness or entropy. Understood in a literal way, when I do something good for another, they are in turn uplifted and express generosity or happiness or goodness sometime later that day. Extrapolating out, I could see that lifetime after lifetime, the stream of momentum gets extraordinarily complex, every action—like the jewels in Indra's Net—reflects every other action, sending shimmers down in a limitless web of cosmic interconnectedness and endless becoming.

Grasping onto a solid sense of self, with all the hurt, fear, anger, and unfinished business that I found myself clinging to so tightly, just ended up letting me justify my negative reactions to myself. It was never going to release me into freedom. When we die, we leave behind everything we've accumulated—possessions, relationships, self-image. The way I was seeing it, our very strong sense of self would, as death appeared, become translucent and then transparent as we transitioned out of this life and merged with undifferentiated consciousness, to form into seed, and then materialize again. Clinging to anything, reacting unskillfully through anger or greed, couldn't possibly help but it was not a sin, it simply showed that one had not penetrated deeply enough into this reality of impermanence or constant change, (anicca), and into emptiness of solid existence, anatta. That clinging to falsity and the unskillful reactions is creates our confusion and suffering (dukkha). Ultimately, wisdom releases us from grasping and gives insight into the fundamental nature of things. Then all that unpleasantness doesn't stick to us, and when we don't get our hands in that gooey mess, we are much less likely to flail about and create a ton of suffering for ourselves and others. I liked the logic and consistency. My mind likes to make sense of things. This was why I was walking. Contemplating as I moved, watching impermanence could lead to simple but profound insight into interconnectedness and emptiness, and with insight, the whole messy construct of psychological pain could resolve. Logical but not easy. I was a little like those 3-D models when you pull apart the layers, they all make sense, just not integrated into one whole self.

As I walked, characters from my childhood appeared in my mind's eye. Past attachments, guilt, and humiliations raised their heads like lake fish popping up to snap at the surface flies. Surrounded by the visual monotony of rocks and snow, water and sky, memory dug into itself and unearthed complex civilizations. The inhabitants, long turned to dust, still rattled around with ghostly presence. In the clarified air, I watched it all arise. Like Siddhartha, I kept my fingers metaphorically touching the ground, as the earth is my witness, I will not move until I penetrate into the true nature of all things. Emotionally, it was a lot. I kept walking. The strength of my memories dissipated. Before I knew it, I was covering ground with each step in the present tense, awake and attentive to the life around me. My pack lightened without all the baggage of my past and I felt tall and agile, strong and content. One small victory, some moments of mindful awareness strung on that vast mala of the path.

I reached the village of Jildo by late afternoon after walking across a great ocean of jet black stones. It seemed to be a dry lakebed, the rocks smooth and unlike those on the mountainsides.

The mountain peaks disappeared into the low clouds, their hues and formations surreal. The houses blended into the terrain; the entire village invisible until I stumbled onto it. Above the wall of an unfinished house, mountain curves smoothed by the fresh snowfall spiraled. The village, made up of about fifteen houses, was just outside Ringdom Gompa, one of the largest monasteries in the area. Such towns were little enclaves of yak sheds, three-sided roofless stone structures, and small two-story houses covered with mud stucco. I had been walking for seven hours, several longer than I had thought it would take. The knot in my shoulder had come back, searing with knifelike intensity and I was grateful for the chance to rest. As I neared, I saw a child, no older than six or seven, huddling against the wind in a yak stall, cradling an even littler one. He was singing and talking to the baby, happy.

Tashi, the househead, came around the corner and invited me in. He was a young man, quiet and gentle with his three small children. His wife had gone to visit her parents in another village. Summertime was a common vacation time, even for women in Zanskar. His children were lovely imps, always singing, dancing, and playing games of jacks or hopscotch in the courtyard. The younger children rode piggyback on the older ones, whose tiny bare feet were hardened against the frozen ground. Runny-nosed and dirty in the cold, they were nonetheless so light-hearted. They interspersed their work with laughter and teasing. Though they ate little, they were strong and healthy and well-loved by their father.

Tashi and his ten-year-old son Sonam were working to construct a new house. They hauled large rocks down the mountainside and piled them into walls, using mud for mortar. The boy worked hard next to his father, wielding a shovel larger than he was. He sliced dirt from the ground and mixed it with water. Each shovelful weighed more than ten kilograms, but he smiled up at his father, who deftly threw the prepared mud against the rocks and smoothed it to a neat stucco finish. I helped load stones for a bit, which was harder work than it looked, rough and cold on the hands. Building together felt good, there was a rhythm and a peace to it.

Their house was typical of the area, with two enclosed

floors and a roof which was fully utilized in the summer months. The first-floor rooms housed the black wooly yaks. Keeping the animals below the living quarters helped to heat the house in the winter. For meals, we sat on small wool carpets around the wood stove which was made of metal and had a pipe chimney to draw the smoke out. The windows looked out over the milking area and let in the eastern morning light. I was bedded in a room used for storage and churning, where a ten-gallon wooden bucket stood next to a support pole. Cloth straps were slung around the pole and the churning stick was pulled, side to side, to churn the fat out of the milk. I woke early in the morning to the sloshing of the liquid and Tashi's eighteen-year-old sister humming. She was blossoming into her beauty, her cheeks reddened from the yak butter she smeared on when she went into the sun. A distracted look settled on her face as she began to sing the words to a romantic ballad. In her daydreams, she churned too quickly, and the bucket tipped, pouring its contents close to my sleeping roll. Tashi rushed in and slapped her, leaving her to run out, humiliated. She stayed out of the house all during breakfast. Tashi prepared the tea and paba, a mixture of tsampa and sho, and called out the window for her. Still ashamed, she did not appear. Tashi sent her sister out to fetch her. As soon as she came and sat with everyone, peace was restored to the household and Tashi looked at her fondly and chuckled.

I spent the morning with an old neighbor who was spinning and carding wool. I pondered the spools and weights hanging about ten feet off the ground but could not understand how her turning of the spools spun the fluff into an even, unbroken strand. She smiled and sang to me, speaking in words that were kind but incomprehensible. The younger children pranced by and jumped onto her bent back. She scolded them, but they only giggled and snuggled their faces into her belly. With thin gnarled hands, she lifted them off and planted smooth round pebbles in front of them. They began an earnest game of Zanskari jacks and she returned to her wobbling spools.

After the evening meal, Tashi's sister brought out the family headdresses for me to try on. They were modest, but when the turquoise studded headpiece was laid on my head, my neck bent under the weight. The ear flaps smelled of yak and I laughed. My features could never be as delicate and graceful as one of these women. I looked at the girl's earnest almond eyes and dark round face and handed the real beauty back her jeweled headdress. We climbed up the ladder to the roof to bring in the drying cheese for the night. In the summer months, the curd and whey are separated, and the curd dried and cured over days into hard little nuggets of cheese. These were perfect travelling food and kept throughout the sparse winter months.

The prayer flags on the roof flapped in the chill wind, sending off a constant stream of mantras down the valley. Around the edges of the roof, bundles of the thin twigs of wild rose bushes were stacked. From the ground, each house looked as though it was alive and growing hair. The stars painted the sky white. I looked off down the dark valley, knowing I must set off again. A sigh rose from within me. If only I could settle down into a loving family. I envied these girls their constancy, they knew the animals and the seasons. They sang together and courted fine men and were cared for by their families. Wouldn't it be nice to stay in one of these houses, to live out a cold winter with chang and prayers? I felt sad that something inside me wanted to see the rest of the valley, compelled to journey and not to settle, to continue the sporadic life of a wanderer seeing others at home, welcomed in while knowing that none of these homes and their constancy and comfort would be mine. What was I looking for? What did I hope to find? I had no goal I could put into words, and I was compelled to continue. I passed a bittersweet night. In the morning, I gave Tashi my cleanest navy-blue L.L. Bean shirt, a small amount of money for whatever they might need, and a pang in my heart. The pull of our goodbyes lingered in me for a long time.

Be like an island, work hard, be wise!
When your impurities are blown away,
and you are free from guilt,
you will enter into the heavenly world
of the precious Noble Ones.

THE DHAMMAPADA
(2ND CENTURY BCE – 4TH CENTURY CE)

Chapter Five
Blessings & Doubt

The sun melted the snow on the valley floor and on the huge slides of the mountains as I walked all the next morning through ice-cold mush, Rangdom Gompa rising up on my left. I snaked through the stairways to the courtyard. It was puja time. There was a line of monks making torma offerings. They fashioned yak butter, tsampa, and red dye into ritual shapes for an elaborate puja. These offerings to the Buddhas and Bodhisattvas were symbolic of inner offerings, of letting go of attachment, of visualizing one's generosity as vast as the limitless sky.

The monks were gentle and unafraid of having a woman sit with them. This was very different from some of the Hindu temples I had made pilgrimage to in the high mountains in the Parvati Valley in northern Himachal Pradesh, where women were considered defilements and forbidden to enter or get near the priests. I found it welcoming. They chanted mantras as they worked, no idle chatter, just meditation in motion and the intention to pierce through the veil of ignorance, still the dust of the mind, and awaken to profound generosity, abundance, and altruism—the bodhisattva ideal. While I had no doubt most were probably ordinary like me, their practice created a field of aspiration and gentleness, the chants always reminding them of how to frame their view. The message that was cemented in their thoughts was of the truth of impermanence, interconnection, and karma. Their chanting and practice etched the habit of commitment to enlightenment. The cloudy, cold day passed easily in the *gompa*. At the end of the long puja, we all ate *paba*, curd, and some awful thin dal. These monasteries stretched their stores to feed all the monks. They depended on offerings, and in a valley where there was not much to go around, supporting so many gompas with surplus was a commitment and a sacrifice. I was grateful they took me in, appreciating how, even though they had little, they gave easily. I dedicated any merit I might have generated to the benefit of all beings and went on to the next town they'd told me was called Tashi Tongse.

I descended from the gompa and set off over the stone sea. At first, the walking was good, but discouragement and loneliness set in quickly after the warmth of the monastery. Sometimes it was like that for me after a meditation retreat. Emptiness, not the good kind, after the exultation of spirit. Next time I was at a library, I wanted to find realizers who'd written about this. It was not quite the despair of *Saint John of the Cross,* but I experienced this low with such regularity, I figured I couldn't be the only one. I kept walking. The terrain seemed so desolate. I rested often, unsure of my own stamina.

Before me was the ascent to Pensi La, a pass of over 4,400 meters some twenty-five kilometers from the monastery. It was the highest I'd been since my first trek a few months earlier in the Langtang range in Nepal. Langtang was a deciding walk for me, an uplifting time with the crimson rhododendrons in bloom and the happy-go-lucky Nepalis singing and teasing each other along the steep, terraced mountainsides. It was Spring and love and lightness was in the air. At the time, I had just finished my first ten-day retreat at Koppan monastery in the Kathmandu Valley and the trek had been a liberating celebration of my first immersion studying Tsongkhapa's graduated path to awakening. I fell in love with the high mountains, the up and down, the strength in my legs, the immersion in the forests and bamboo at the lower elevations, and the breathtaking vistas above the tree line. Nepal was like the shire where the hobbits lived, lush and lively.

Pensi La was very different. More Zen. The mountains looked like humpback whales breaching the surf, blue-black rock scarred by streaks of white ice and snow. It was quiet. So quiet. No chirping of forests or farmers. Just rock, snow, wind, and the path beneath my feet. The climb to the pass was gradual. The Doda river poured out of the Drang Drung Glacier's mouth and dropped down deep to the east on my right. The valley narrowed and a tunnel of snow mountains on either side hugged me. I headed up. I could feel the air thinning, clarifying, calling for more. It was a paradox, the climb demanded both more focus and more expansion. Too much focus in, I'd lose my way or feel discouraged by the intensity. Too much expansion out, I'd slip and stumble and become dizzy by the heights. Such was the way in meditation as well. Open awareness in meditation creates a sense of sharp, clear, wide open nonrestriction. The spirit can soar, freed from the dead weight of thoughts. In meditation I could just be, neither moving towards nor away from. Walking up to the pass, in spite of the surface layer of my thoughts, I had that same sense of being deeply attentive and nonjudgmental. Neither liking nor disliking, neither bringing together nor dividing.

I loved the mountains fiercely. It was not a love that separated what I cared for from what I didn't. It was Love, without a past or future tense. In that non-division, I could see while not focusing on anything in particular. Usually, there is an in-between, between us and what we see, between us and the atmosphere—whether that be air, identity, or time. Here there was connection all the way through from eye to air to massive glacial wall. As J. Krishnamurti or Vimala Thakar would say, no seer and seen, only the immediacy of seeing. The closeness was overwhelming. I could feel it pressing up against my chest. I flung my arms wide and twirled around, drinking in the whole universe at this particular cosmic inter-section, this point on which I stood, at the nexus between the world and all that is.

I felt so happy I didn't know what to do with myself.

The great thing about trekking is there's nothing else to do. Celebration, discouragement, the next step is still the same. Just keep going. It's like the dharma, I thought. Realize, and continue. The path unfolds, life changes, challenges purify, ascents are scaled, and everything is also perfect as it is. There is no moving, nowhere to get to.

I kept walking. I was surprised and pleased to find a low stone shepherd's hut waiting for me at the top of the pass, which was wide and flat, a rolling passage across a smoothed out hilltop. I collected wild rhubarb stalks for soup and twigs encased in frost for the cooking fire. A clear stream ran nearby and the inside of the hut was clean. A light snow began to fall as the daylight dissipated and I prepared my dinner alone.

From that brief eruption of cosmic passion, my thoughts started to descend. Out of the blue, the silence and solitude started to press in on me. The mountains and glaciers were chanting their rumbling dirge of constant change and instead of comforting, tonight it was feeling low and a little menacing. As I reflected on the day, I didn't quite know how to make sense of these sudden changes, the pendulum swings from an immersion in such beauty and intimacy that all my questions about life were instantly answered to a half day later, suffocated by the clammy mist of undefined fear and self-doubt. Isn't that always the way? We repeatedly search for what we've already found and then feel sad because we can't see it, because it is us, and we can't turn back and separate from it to reflect on our own essence.

The little crackles of the fire cheered me, it had been a long day.

The next morning, the descent from the pass was gradual and the valley widened into lush green pastures. It was welcoming and light and I forgot the shadow in my mind just like a curious pika, those rambunctious Himalayan hares who forget the shadow of the hawk once he wings his way onward. Looking around, I couldn't keep a smile from breaking across my face. The turf was springy and dotted with tiny yellow, white, and blue wildflowers. The wind was low and to my back. I could have flown if only I could have let go of my attachment to earthly things. Beautiful as they were, they bound me to the earth and limited me in my human frame, defined me by my past, my family and their dysfunction, my culture and its dark underbelly, and my experiences that left me confused or inadequate.

It seemed sad to realize beauty and then to perceive that the desire for beautiful things prevented me from truly experiencing them as they were. Did my very love of intricate rock patterns trap me in the cycle of likes and dislikes? Was that what was keeping me from realizing the very harmony I sought? I was confused, caught in a mental game, ensnared by my thought process to discount the joy I was stumbling upon. The texts say that the ego never seeks its own death. The true heart seeks to live life exultant in the One that is never lost, never lonely, never fragmented or separate. But I bounced back and forth between the extremes, I was still trapped in experience, not wizened by the truth those experiences revealed. I trusted my exacting mind and its desire to self-perpetuate. The dominance of my thought process took me down an increasingly frustrating labyrinth of logical nihilism, which went something like this.

What use was it to walk for weeks into an isolated part of the world if I continue to carry the baggage of mental concepts and categories with me? Flight beyond the confines of the usual, the known, entices me, but I don't see how to let go, how to transcend my mind's habit of labeling, conceptualizing, and separating. Pure awareness and present-tense experience demand total allegiance. But I resist! My mind wants room for itself. How could I be without it? I only know how to relate to both a seer and a seen. I only know how to define what non-separation is not. Even if my way of seeing the world is weighting my feet to the ground and my heart to its worries and fears, how can I do otherwise?

The first part of developing discrimination is recognizing one's own ignorance. That always sounded easy to me, but I was finding, it sure smarted. It takes time to renounce the allure of one's own mental gymnastics and let those endless thoughts pass across the screen of awareness like a crappy commercial for a product I would never buy. I was trying to discern real from unreal. And I was carrying so many judgments and criticisms that the unity I desired eluded me again and again.

The next few days I kept walking in and out of this reflection. One night, so many stars shone that the path was illuminated and I could see my own shadow. I walked under the magic until the wee hours of the night. The sky was a jet-black kimono studded with pearls and diamonds, embracing and enfolding the valley. Spirit, not my feet, carried me along. My heart expanded and I became large, no longer encased and defined by my body's tiny boundaries, limitless, at once the heart of the mountains, the tiniest pebble, and the distant star. Love filled me and an ancient song spread a smile on my lips. I felt no will, or desire, or disturbance. In that moment of pristine existence, I caught a glimpse into the nature of things. I did not see the mountains, I became them from inside. I was wide, so big, nothing was excluded. I was the velvet sky looking down on the earth and I was the sand floor of the valley, each minute blossom and every creature. That night, I camped beside a shimmering white stupa and fell into a deep sleep.

Joy is to delight in other's pleasure and success;
It is to cultivate the wish that all have happiness.
It is a joy one feels when they achieve it
for themselves
And is the wish that they should never be deprived
of it.

JIGME LINPA
(1729-1798)

Chapter Six
No Self & Bawdy Woman

Women in these mountains are hardy and self-assured. They were a welcome contrast to the more subservient women of the Indian plains, in many ways they are more familiar to me. But they have a freedom and confidence my culture lacks. They didn't look over their shoulder for reassurance. They moved freely among the men, equal in a way I'd never seen anywhere else in the world; they were accorded respect. Often I witnessed husband and wife sharing household tasks with each other. According to their customs, both men and women may have more than one spouse. I found it more common to meet a woman with several husbands, often marrying their first husband's brothers. It was practical. In the winter months, men would ride their horses up the frozen rivers, sometimes traveling all the way to Turkey. Without another husband, women would be too vulnerable in the austere land. But I felt, in addition to the practical solution, the women really had too much verve, zest, and vital energy to be contained by a single partner. They made me smile.

Several days after descending Pensi La, I came upon three women weeding a field. The plateau was high, hiding the tiny village I thought they called Himling. It wasn't on my map but it existed all the same. The women called me over to them, cooing in their high-pitched mountain voices and grinning mischievously. The look they shot in my direction promised fun and I willingly took up their company. We began plucking weeds side by side, chewing on *arsey*, a lemony grass. They were unkempt and brazen, talking rapidly about something that set the older woman into fits of laughter and the prepubescent nun into vivid blushes. They smelled earthy, and I was taken in by their strength and womanly warmth. Soon they drew me into their fun, making a circle with their forefinger and thumb, and poking the index finger of the other hand through it. Then they poked me in the belly, asking in a universal language, "Do you do it?"

They were curious and without shyness, but I felt my face grow warm and I grinned. I may have appeared strange in their eyes, but we were all women and knew the pleasures of love. They quickly jabbed my breasts and pinched my nipples through my wool pheran with their coarse brown fingers. The young nun rolled on the small barley shoots in paroxysms of laughter. Through their jest, our differences melted away and the strangeness between us vanished. They were astounded at the hair that grew long on my legs. Their people bore very little hair on their bodies which seemed backwards to me. In such a frigid climate, I would expect them to have grown thick body hair, but instead, they were smooth-skinned where the people of hot climates like the Mediterranean were thick furred.

Since I was to be their guest for the night, and, they hoped, for quite some days, at least until the husband of the house returned from the wedding he was attending in Padum, it was an occasion to call off work early. I mentioned my hunger and we all trooped down to their house in the village to begin a long evening of tea, tsampa, and chapatis. The living space was tiny, they seemed to be one of the poorer families in the village and the middle-aged woman had a gaggle of five small children. Unlike the other houses I had been to, this one was dirty; the wooden window was sloppily fitted, and grimy cups and plates were scattered on the sleeping rugs which jumped with bedbugs and lice. My host grabbed an ewe's rear legs and dragged her to a bucket to donate strong-smelling sheep's milk for their special guest. She sang silly songs and the nun shyly told a tale about the Buddha, which I was beginning to be able to follow, having heard enough of the same words in the teachings and retreats and checking my little notebook for my ad hoc dictionary, created conversation by conversation. The children wrestled too close to the fire, dusting our tea with ashes. They would have kept me up all night had I let them, but it had been a long day traveling at such heights and my lids were drooping. Drolka urged me to stay, the esteemed regional astrologer was to come through their village. There was a schoolteacher to meet and songs to learn. My mind spun with all these thoughts and itched like my bug-bitten skin.

I turned towards the little shelf that held seven brass altar bowls and thanked Buddha for the hearth and bosom of this woman's household, grateful for the bonding and the honesty. Whether Easterner or Westerner, our natures were all the same, and we could find a common language and much wisdom if we cared to meet across the divides. We met as curious girls, in trust and fun. As I opened my heart in thanks, the nun curled up on special carpets by the warm side of the fire. Drolka closed the wooden door and untied the sash of her outer garment, spreading the cloak over the children and herself. Her breath soon sighed heavily with sleep but, tired as I was, I continued to stare at the black forms in the room and at the stars that fought through the cracks in the window, not knowing where to deposit my excess wonderment. Such a small pleasure, telling ribald stories with another woman, sharing food and songs, and sleeping next to one another. In which of these mundane actions had I ever before found myself overflowing with gratitude and what I must call blessing? This must be the stuff blessings were made off, not expensive gifts coveted and received, not achievements planned out and accomplished, but a meeting of hearts for no reason, for no end but laughter and joy. The blessing was in the experiencing, whatever the specifics might be, without wishing to prolong, manipulate, or structure an interaction towards one's own will. Grace flows in living without grasping.

I wanted to preserve my joy so that it might not be lost when this happy feeling passed. The Tibetans have a practice where they dedicate their merits to all sentient beings, sharing any benefits they may be entitled to with all others. They reason this way, if one has a cup of water and leaves it in the sun, the water will quickly evaporate and the cup will become dry as a bone. But if one takes that same cup of water and pours it into a lake, the waters merge as one and one's own source is never dry. I closed my eyes and breathed deeply, feeling the calm and energy flowing through me. I wished peace upon all other creatures, sending messages out to those known and unknown to me, those of this realm and the realms I had yet to see. Pouring my blessings into the ocean of all that existed, I slipped into sleep.

Much as I wanted to stay with them, I knew that one day could easily become ten and I felt propelled to keep walking. The astrology predictions would have to wait for another time. I said my goodbyes over a quick morning tea. Everyone accepted the parting without fuss or bother. It was good to be out in the open, moving, letting it all flow.

It turned out to be an odd day. The trail was practically congested and I crossed paths with an odd parade of people every few hours. First, I met three Belgian men had been walking a similar route but from the reverse direction. They had come south from Lamayuru but decided to take an inside track, avoiding Padum. It had been extremely difficult for them. They told me Dras had fifteen meters of snow. They had forded frigid rivers with waters running waist high and were trailed by snowstorms. They shared that it was possible to reach Lamayuru if I took the route through Padum. I was encouraged. That was the path I was on. A few hours later I met up with a German and Englishman trekking in from Manali to do, of all things, a photoshoot of men's suits on the high passes. I never expected I'd encounter that in the middle of those rock-bare mountains! My final meeting was with a Sardinian and German hippie couple, Andrea and Peter, who were even less prepared than I was but who were used to living rough on the India circuit. They argued more than they got along and I was glad to be traveling on my own. We were all such an odd cast of characters, each with our own stories. I wondered what karmic entanglement crossed our paths at this time, in this most unlikely of places, for these brief but warming encounters. There was some kind of message to it all that I couldn't see. But, for now, I felt renewed energy flow through me, revitalized by our conversations and happy to be able to speak my own language and to converse in more than just half sentences.

That night, I found a shepherd's roofless stone house and settled in for the night. It was a restless one and I woke at five to a light snowstorm. I packed up quickly, wondering if it was time to leave behind the Anaïs Nin book that was weighing down my pack. Sometimes she made me cry and sometimes she gave me courage as I searched for my own expression. She moved on the edges, and I was now on my own. Next opportunity, I decided, I'd pass the book on.

*The three worlds are as impermanent as the clouds
of autumn. The births and deaths of beings are like
watching a dance.
The speed of human's lives is like lightning in the sky;
It passes as swiftly as a stream down a steep
mountain.
When his time comes, even a king will die,
And his wealth, friends, and relatives cannot follow
him.
But wherever people go, wherever they remain,
Karma, like a shadow, will follow after them.*

PADMASAMBHAVA
(8TH CENTURY CE)

Chapter Seven
Accepting the Wheel of Life

Around midday the next day, a horseman passed me bearing important messages to the king of Zanskar. He was young and flirtatious and offered me a ride on the back of his white barrel-bellied pony. The small beast bore his burden well, two riders and my pack, and his hooves made quick work of the upwards climb. Zanskari ponies are renowned for their sure-footedness, endurance, and capacity to withstand cold and high elevations. In the wintertime, when the rivers freeze over with their thick ice covers, locals from all corners of the valley travel to Leh for winter pujas and trading. The rivers follow the most direct course and, with a fast pony, a winter journey could take a fraction of the time of summer travel.

My companion seemed anxious to make time and he left me when we reached the shiny metal bridge spanning the river near Phe. I was happy to dismount, the rear quarters of the horse were a bit wider than my hips were accustomed to stretching, and his ardent advances, though harmless, had grown tiresome. He deposited me into the hands of an elderly woman and her granddaughter who were on their way to Padum for a wedding celebration. The day dimmed and with smiles they pushed me to hurry my pace. From where we were I could make out the tin roofs of Indian army barracks.

I guessed that Padum would follow close on the heels of the camp but it seemed far and my feet were leaden.

The way carried many people. Villages grew closer together and green stretched out on the valley floor. Here in the wide valley with so much sun, the barley was already knee-high and the dal perfumed the way with its delicate yellow flowers. Drolma, my companion, spotted her sister, coming down the path towards us. They met with excited greetings and affectionate pats on the shoulder.

"Jullay! Jullay!" they called to each other. Drolma asked her sister how she was getting along.

She burst into a torrent of tears. "Life is so hard, so hard. How am I to survive without my husband? For so many years he was by my side but now he has left his body and the bad winds are blowing through me. I cannot work. Oh, what am I to do?" She moaned and wailed, her cries bouncing off the rock cliffs with eerie echoes.

Drolma drew her sister close. "Tshh, tshhh," she soothed, "We are both of us old ladies. Stop carrying on like this. We all must die; this is the unfolding of life. Just as we have changed bodies infinite times before, we will continue to roll around this wheel of births and deaths until we are able, through our wisdom and merit, to break the cycle of suffering. Have you no understanding? Pray for a better rebirth for Tsering. Surely he amassed great merit in this life through his prayers and study and good deeds. This will follow him into the next life. Tshh, tshh. You are sad, he was a good man to you but if you persist with these wrong views of self-pity and attachment you will disturb his smooth passage and you will create the causes for rebirth for yourself in the lower realms. Go and make an offering to the Lamas and ask them to prescribe some mantras to drive the bad winds out of you. Now we must continue on our journey. The blessings of Buddha be upon you." She stroked the cheek of her sister gently. They smiled and clasped hands.

Two wrinkled old women who had passed many births and deaths, many furious winters and succulent harvests. Once they had been young girls with thick black braids

54

and an itch in their limbs, teasing and giggling. What had become of those young bodies? What remained of the two girls, now old women?

We all must age. None of us can escape the march of time. No one can escape death. Yet we cling to our lives with a white-knuckled grip and deny the natural cycles within and around us. I was attached to the supple and strong body of my youth and denied my perishability. Would I be caught like others, shocked by the changes that might occur while my head was turned, nose buried in the emotions and activities of the present, without reflection or wisdom? The infant grows into a girl and the girl develops into a mother. The mother, now an old lady, looks at the coming of her death. In the midst of all the variation, what remains the same? What can I point my finger at and say, "This is me"? Even the great mountains change from season to season, the rivers become solid and then liquid, the water circulates constantly, and glaciers rumble their slow gait down the slopes. How can creatures as small as we continue to live in the fantasy that our bodies and our lives will never change when even the vast sky above us wears a new face every moment? Does the sky mourn the loss of its rain clouds? No. But we do. We cling to our ignorance and suffer when change takes from us something or someone we have grown to rely on.

Drolma walked with brisk, light steps, humor in her eyes. "Ahh teh, she was always one to make a fuss. In this, she hasn't changed." She reached over and pinched her granddaughter. "You too will become an old lady like us, do not smile too smugly. Remember to recite your mantras, make offerings, and be kind to all sentient beings. Acquire much merit in this life, for though we all must die, we can create the causes for a more fortunate rebirth. Avoid all bad actions which will yield the karma for a next life in one of the hell realms. Om mani padme hum. Om mani padme hum. Om mani padme hum." She clicked the rosewood beads of her mala, marking mantras as our steps raised small clouds of dust.

After a few hours, we came to a village and Drolma offered to take me to the house of one of her friends where I could bed for the night. The woman she brought me to made me gasp, she was such a regal beauty. She was tall—more than a foot taller than the women who accompanied me—and had a long and angular nose that seemed almost Grecian. Her complexion was light with a faint rose blush on her cheeks, not the coarse and sunburnt skin of the other villagers. Her tapered fingers wrote poems in the air with each movement and her movements were like deliberate statements, powerful dances. Her obvious means showed in her immaculate black cloak, Chinese silk blouse, and shiny silk tophat.

The living room was spacious. Newly stuccoed walls shone cleanly, displaying framed photographs of family members and His Holiness the Dalai Lama. The brass on her chai gurgur gleamed. She led me into a guest room, newly constructed, with windows on two walls looking out over verdant fields and a raised bed covered with wool carpets. The dust on my tattered shoes shamed me. I burned with awkwardness, aware of my thin and unkempt hair and sweat-stained collar in the reflection of her smooth neck shining with strands of pink seed pearls. We withdrew into the living room, and she motioned for me to sit on the ornate dragon carpets around the iron woodstove. She offered sugar tea, a sign of unusual means, and listed a menu I had hardly dreamt about in these parts. Where was I?

Then it dawned on me. This was no extraordinary invitation, but a high-class hotel close to Padum, the capital of the district, ready to receive many visitors when the road was opened. I realized she must cater not only to army officials but also to the few wealthy European climbing groups who came this way. Her hospitality was a business venture and, when I inquired, her rates were high for someone like me. I lived with limited means, when I was in the mountains or staying in a small village for a stretch, I could keep my budget to fifteen dollars a month. I fully intended to stretch what I had for as many months or years as I could. Much as I was impressed and somewhat intimidated by her grace and beauty, it wasn't the moment to run up a bill that would cover a night on the town in New Delhi.

During my travels so far in the valley, I'd been the recipient of so much generosity it was overwhelming. I had been given gifts of food and lodging. I tried to reciprocate but this easy hospitality was the way of the Zanskari. They give now for they will be recipients later. Karma, what goes around comes around. Self-sufficient and generous, people took care of one another. In this sustainable economy, wealth for one did not come at the expense of another, prosperity was shared.

While not wanting to exploit my hosts' hospitality and limited resources, I often struggled with how to be. In Nepal, I had seen wealthy trekkers move into precariously balanced mountain regions and destroy the local economy, crudely running over the gentility of the local people or un-balancing the relative equality of means with a massive infu-sion of cash. Westerners, with our acculturated materialism and progress-oriented bias, implanted greed and competition into environments that, for generations, had been sustained by cooperation and generosity. Westerners as role models made a show of argumentation, criticism, impatience, and anger that, unfortunately, many Nepalis had begun to imitate. In fact, since a French filmmaker shot a television series in Ladakh that was broadcast throughout Europe, the region had become a popular area for eclectic and wealthy travelers and the im-pact had not been favorable.

For thousands of years Zanskar has been a sustain-able economy, with a stable population level, sufficient but not excessive arable land, and a rhythm and balance that created contentment and joy. While local people here could benefit from simple cataract procedures, solar light, wind-based irri-gation methods, and other Western innovations, their lifestyle was precious, balanced, and advanced. On a human level, in terms of quality of life and fulfillment, their culture was like nothing I had ever experienced before. Ladakh had no records of murders at the time I visited, but since westerners began to visit with more regularity, the area had witnessed a num-ber of violent, even fatal, altercations. An instant and unequal flow of cash into a basically moneyless economy upends the natural balance. Long-term village harmony can be broken quickly when even just one villager opens a dry goods store at prices fit for travelers and not for locals.

I felt uneasy before realizing that I could simply carry on my way. I finished my tea and tactfully explained that I hoped to make it to Padum that evening and would go on. Her demeanor changed little if at all and I felt none of the sales pressure that often accompanied business transactions in India. I wished her well in her endeavor. I was sure she would profit handsomely from climbing tours and wealthy tourists who paid handsomely to venture into the mountains. I hoped she maintained her integrity and equanimous Buddhist nature. I hoped the manners of my countrymen were influenced by the stoic Zanskari culture and not the other way around. While impermanence is a basic teaching in Buddhism, so is the commitment to evolve our ways of living and to not devolve or feed the lower natures of greed, anger, and attachment. Colonization and industrialization are causing one of the greatest extinctions on the planet: the erasure of cultures, languages, and ways of life that naturally arose in harmony with their own environments. I fear for the erosion of this life, and with it the loss of these people's joy.

America, even given her noble ideals of liberty and the pursuit of happiness, often felt empty and harsh on her people, which was why I had traveled halfway around the world in the first place: to learn how to integrate this other way of being into my own—their joy and ease, their confidence and strength, their wisdom and faith. My search for enlightenment had brought me here and I felt nourished in dimensions of my being I hadn't even realized were parched and dry. I was indebted to these people. They gave me far more than I gave to them. They taught me lessons I could never have learned in college at Cornell.

But what about my impact here? My very presence created a dilemma I didn't know how to solve or judge. There were no easy answers. The effects of European encroachment were unsettling. I wished Zanskar could remain as it always had been. Yet I too was responsible for this change. As sensitive as I tried to be, I was one of those materialists, bringing nylon with me into a world that knew homespun wool. I had come to learn new-old ways but I carried myself with modern industrialized judgments, habits, and, much as I was reluctant to admit it, values. I traveled alone, hauling my own gear, yet I still stuck out with my embarrassing pride. Could I justify my footprint, balance my intrusion? Were my steps, like other seekers, eroding Shangrila, while we saw ourselves developing wisdom to uplift our world? Every traveler helped open the way, one by solitary one, until a thoroughfare to the remote Himalayas is built. There are so few remaining frontiers.

This contemplation confused and upset me. If my commitment was clear seeing, then I had no choice but to accept my impact, see my aversion to change, and bear responsibility for my involvement in that change. I struggled with the puzzle pieces. I couldn't help the world without more depth and dimensionality. I pursued awakening, but was my time in the mountains necessary or self-serving? The truest heights to climb and wastelands to cross are in one's own being. Still, for thousands of years, yoginis had gone to the mountains to simplify and reach a quality of being beyond the ordinary. They were drawn, as I was, to separate from the momentum of worldly existence, let the elevation loosen the weight of a troubled and cloudy mind. So I wrestled internally. And I walked.

After lunching in Phe, I continued my journey across the cold stone valley past Sani into a small village. Tucked next to the village was its temple. Dating back to sometime around 127 AD, during the reign of Kanishka, a powerful emperor and early adherent of Buddhism, it is believed to be the oldest in the region. Though hard to know for sure, two of the most highly accomplished realizers are said to have spent years meditating here, Padmasambhava or Guru Rinpoche and Naropa. I generally felt a strong connection to Guru Rinpoche, with his wildness, his wandering, and his meditative feats. There was a stillness in the area. A hush. The cold and the rock floor quieted my mind.

I had few thoughts at this point but I needed rest. Though I felt not quite up to staying in a village I was too spent to find a suitable camp spot. The valley was wide, and it would mean a long walk to the shelter of the mountains on either side. The ground was strewn with rocks. In the approaching evening, a chill was coming into the air. I walked on to the village, a bit despondent. Crowds of children and adults came out to greet me. I smiled weakly.

Good fortune was with me and the family that invited me in were quiet and peaceful people. They knew without me needing to tell them that it had been a long day and they gently brought me into their house. They murmured to the children to be quiet and showed me into my room for the night. I set up my bedroll and joined them by the fire, taking in the scene around me. Husband and wife knelt side by side and prepared thukpa, a thin broth with tsampa noodles. It was comforting seeing them cook together, still a little surprising seeing their egalitarian home. I had become accustomed to the Indian way of life, where the food preparation is solely a woman's occupation, where the man of the house often ate first, then the children, and then the women had whatever was left over.

This house was spacious and dim, a quintessential Zanskari home. The inner room where we sat was surrounded by other smaller rooms, keeping it insulated during the long, cold winter months. It was mid-July, and the night would have been bitter had I ended up sleeping under the stars. Four doors led off the main room, in the center of which was a one-meter square opening to the roof. This allowed smoke to escape and gave access by way of a notched pole ladder to the stores of firewood ringing the rooftop. Two crossed birch logs blackened by soot supported the twig ceiling. These were supported by four smaller vertical pillars which served to divide the room into four areas. In the southeast corner of the room was the clay fireplace, which had no chimney, and two wooden crates containing the odd ladle, cups, and boxes. Along the wall hung many other ladles of different shapes and sizes with triangular flat ends, a shelf with kerosine wick lamps, and old milk tins filled with salt teas and tsampa. Also hanging off the shelf was a Ladakhi bow, mirror, leather pouch possibly containing medicines, and a chai gurgur. At the north end of the room hung cloths, extra clothes, and two colorful dharma coats used for special festivals.

Stuck into the ceiling was an old black Indian umbrella, and several large balls of wool, hanging down like oversized spider-egg sacs. Some large spinning spools lay on the floor next to a ten-gallon water pot made of fine copper. Near an open door were children's blankets, and a wooden frame used as a sort of pillow. Above them hung two more maroon wool coats and a white fleece wrap. The wall was cut with another door, leading into a pitch-dark room. Beside this was a wicker basket covered with a white cloth on top of which cheese was drying, a 25-gallon water cauldron standing in a wooden frame, several wooden milk buckets, and more pots, ladles, and brooms. Another doorway was beside this, the exit to the stairs leading to the lower stables, the toilet room, and the room where I was staying.

Their daughter, little Jamyang, who had a beautiful, happy face, sang softly to herself. She couldn't have been more than three years old and twirled and danced like a ballerina in bare feet. Her father came over and hugged her, then wiped her nose. How these parents cared for their children! A small gesture like that, wiping a running nose, was common and the affection was tangible and warm. Jamyang chased the sparrows out of the room, tongue hanging out of her mouth like a coddled spaniel and her father left the fireside to rock the restless baby hidden under the mound of blankets. He spoke in a low voice, murmuring a soft lullaby. His wife made thick yellow chapatis and then we all got ready for bed.

I spent a restless night with piercing stomach cramps. Dysentery or something with all the same symptoms had returned. I had spent many months in Nepal plagued with diarrhea, dehydration, and fever, but the invariant diet of tsampa, salt, and butter had either clogged up or cleaned out my system. I woke, embarrassed, having peed a little in my sleep from the cold. I couldn't find my way to the toilet room in the dark. In most houses, they kept one room empty, with a hole leading to a floor below where there was a pile of dirt and a shovel. Every day, fresh dirt or straw was put on top of the night soil from an outside entrance. When it has composted, it was mixed with straw and dung and used to fertilize the fields.

Sometimes, when my bowels were not functioning regularly and the cold air made my bladder loose, whimpers, like those of a lost child rose up in my throat. Clutching at the cramps in my stomach, I ached for home and an easy-to-find western bathroom with a toilet, toilet paper, running hot water, and soap. I rocked myself back into dreams of a home. I was unsettled, with a deep tiredness in my soul. It had been a long journey thus far, about 230 kilometers, and not always easy. Sometimes the strangeness, the isolation, and the differences were frightening. Cut off from people by custom and habitat, language and religion, I sometimes felt so alone in spite of everyone's warmth. They were in their homes with their families. I was far, in distance and in spirit, from anyone I could call family or any home that felt like somewhere I could be. Disease is a leveler. When illness comes the exoticism and thrill of the journey evaporate. The elevation and thin air— geographically and spiritually—which usually exhilarated me now made me feel thin and uneasy.

I wondered if it might be the influence of the black magic of the region, drawn to my foreign presence, that laid these moods on me. I'd seen symbols tied from the corners of the houses, masks of bird or goat skulls with leather tassels and feathers. They would rustle a little in the wind, eerie protectors. The region was supposedly filled with practitioners of the black magic side of the Bon religion. I saw charcoal lines drawn over a child's face in another village to make him ugly and undesirable to the demons. I had noticed this practice among the Hindus in the plains, too, especially when they had lost a child. Bon, a predecessor of Tibetan Buddhism, had developed a subtle and refined system of meditation, esoteric and tantric practices, spells and incantations, and exorcisms. The adepts were said to be able to pacify bad spirits invading an area or a household, expel demons from a misfortunate individual, and even control the winds and the rain to help harvests. It was a world I didn't understand but that felt alive. I felt I could easily walk into a tripwire unsuspectingly and set off a misfortunate chain of events. Perhaps that was the shadow I felt out of nowhere, affecting me but unclear whether it was coming from inside or out.

It also could have been the play of altitude sickness, which I had never bothered to learn enough about. Headaches, blurred vision, disorientation, trouble sleeping, and nausea were all symptoms. I wasn't sure whether altitude sickness was caused by the decrease in air pressure at higher altitudes or by a decrease in the concentration of oxygen, but I knew it was common in mild forms from as low as 2,000 meters above sea level. Meanwhile, I was walking at a base of 3,000 meters and only going up. Any of these were possible, I was much more inclined to believe that I was working out past *samskaras*, negative karmic imprints from unskillful actions in past lifetimes. To me, that made more sense and was more useful that assuming the shadows that crossed my heart and weakened my body were from some atmospheric, amoebic, or chemical change. Anyway, I decided, it could be those samskaras that made me prone to altitude sickness in the first place. When you are alone with your own mind, you do the best you can. I thought a little more, and dozed off to sleep.

Venerable Ananda said to The Buddha,
"Half of this holy life, Lord, is good and noble friends,
companionship with the good, association with the
good."

"Do not say that, Ananda!" replied The Buddha.
"It is the whole of this holy life,
this friendship, companionship
and association with the good.

When a renunciate has admirable people
as friends, companions, and comrades,
they can be expected to develop
and pursue the noble eightfold path."

THE BUDDHA
(5TH CENTURY BCE)

Chapter Eight
Just One Snap in a Sari!

The difficult night passed and I found myself approaching the bustling "metropolis" of the region, Padum. In comparison to towns I had crossed with some twenty or thirty houses, this was like a city, with multiple streets, barracks, and Indian administrative offices. Padum was a crossroads with Manali in the south, Kargil in the northwest, and Leh in the northeast. It saw trade, military, international security interests, and interstate trading opportunities. It sprawled across the floor of a wide valley in a cluster of houses, home to some 700 people out of the 12,000 in Zanskar overall. The mountains edging the u-shaped valley were of medium height and enclosed a desert. I walked over soft sand and stones and some prickly desert plants. A strong wind swept light dust everywhere. I turned a corner and suddenly the town was hidden somewhere to my right. The houses blended in with the stone mountains, though occasionally I caught the glint of light on the tin roofs. It was hard to say how far it was.

When I reached Padum in the very late afternoon, Moti, a banker, invited me into his home. He and his wonderful wife Krishna were Kashmiri Hindus who had been sent to Padum three years prior by the Indian government. Krishna spoke English fairly well and clearly showed how delighted she was to meet a woman with whom she could converse. She told me, in a husky but hushed voice, how difficult it had been for her, isolated by long winters and as the only Hindu woman in the village. She couldn't speak to the Buddhists, and besides, she said, they drank too much chang. As a woman, she found little company among the Muslim villagers, made up forty percent of the population of Padum. They were more circumspect about the mingling of the genders and she neither fit in with the men or women. Still, she was jolly and good natured about it all. She was delighted with the few tikas, red beauty dots for the forehead, that I had to give her. When I left, I also gave her my faded bra from America which really pleased her. She cooked succulent vegetarian Indian food for me, subji, chawal, dal, mint curd, and chutney, and we talked.

Krishna cut a sculpted, stoic figure. She had a lovely long oval face like many Kashmiris and large white teeth. She moved quietly behind her jovial, paunch-bellied husband but her voice belied all the strength and independence inside her. She called a hearty greeting to all the children we passed in the streets. Although it was obvious they were a love match, she had no children of her own and so she shared everything with Moti in that barren land. Perhaps because of the isolation, she was able to participate more in financial and work matters than if she had remained in Kashmir. I admired her. In her being was the proud strength and independence that rarely showed in public among Kashmiri women, but when it did, it was outstanding. She was generous to her servants and kind to the street urchins. Hasan, their house help who seemed to enjoy as leisurely a pace as he could get away with, was equally treated to biscuits closely rationed by Krishna and the festive chutneys she prepared for us. He also sat in on the history and science lessons that Moti taught to two local boys and was well versed in the goings-on of the town.

After dinner, we walked through the beautiful dusk along the river to Narayin, the second banker's house. He was also Kashmiri and Moti and Krishna's closest friend. We gossiped and talked politics and spirituality in English until after 10 p.m. and walked back under the deep canopy of night. The mountains were multicolored and magnificent. I looked around at our entourage, which included Narayin and a few neighbors we picked up along the way, together we were Kashmiri Hindus, a Sikh, a Muslim, a Buddhist, and an American Jew. I chuckled to myself at our little inter-religious convocation in the rarified air of Zanskar.

A rocky, jeepable road had been constructed from Kargil to Padum a couple of years earlier to help connect the Indian government to such a strategic area but not much remained of the road after the year's particularly severe winter. Krishna, with sad eyes, told me that the road had closed on October 29 and now, July 14, it was still closed. Supplies were not expected to come through until mid-August. All the government stores in the town were locked and deserted. I found only one hotel willing to sell sugar but at four times the normal cost. I had been counting on replenishing my food stores, candles, and other small supplies there, as was everyone else in town.

New hotels were sprouting up all over with the promise of the road and increased tourism, but none of them had been completed yet. That year, fewer tourists than hoped for had descended on Padum. Still, they had come, with sunburned noses, wind-cracked lips, and bulky cameras. So large and clumsy they seemed beside the wide-faced and compact Zanskari. I spoke a little with some trekkers arriving from Manali but was relieved to be able to retreat to my Indian household. Their western assertiveness and over-confidence were a bit much for me and I found myself with little to say.

I decided to take a couple more days rest in my temporary home. It turned out to be a good time to let the wave of trekkers make their way through. The next day, I heard commotion in the streets and went up to the roof, where I stood gaping, like all the other villagers, at a Sierra Club group marching through town. It was one of the group's first treks to the area. There were eighteen Americans, thirteen horses, and a passel of guides and cooks. Their presence was quickly broadcast throughout the town thanks to their bright-colored Gore-tex jackets, hiking boots, and extra running shoes hanging off their nylon daypacks. I heard loud voices and New York accents.

Moti sent me out to speak with them and see if they had anything to sell. In his quiet way, he made quite a business buying knick-knacks from western trekkers for his own use or to sell at higher prices back in Kashmir. I reluctantly agreed. I wanted to protect my escape from my own culture. I saw the tourists as intruders, not just in the valley but in my mental space, my pilgrimage away from the materialism, small-mindedness, and ambition that made the west so enticing and so disappointing. The tourists I met in the valley were not nearly as nice as the locals. Like on any meditation retreat, they became fun-house mirrors for some of my own issues and qualities. I went down to the center of town and ended up spending a couple hours with the group, hearing stories and news. They told me that a Swiss man had had really bad altitude sickness at Pensi La and that their guide was here radioing for a helicopter to rescue him. A good reminder. These are heights with real dangers, respect and caution was so necessary. I didn't find any extra shoes for Moti, but I was generously given an extra set of batteries for my camera which I desperately needed. Overall, the individuals were nice but like many groups, they seemed more interested in talking about their experience than listening. That was fine with me, I wasn't sure I wanted to share that much of the special places and people I'd met with such a hurried and large mountain tour.

That evening, as I lay in bed, I wondered how accurate my perception was of the Zanskaris or whether I just didn't understand their language well enough. Maybe I would have found them greedy and selfish too if I had been able to understand them better, but my sense was that they were much less so, tempered by their beliefs and practice. They were raised with an education that helped them deal with life, understanding a broader context and the profound interrelationship of all things. Without denying any feelings within the human emotional range and without placing too much importance on anything that was bound by its nature to change, they lived by the teaching that each of us has a Buddha nature, the capacity for a clear mind or awakened consciousness. We just need to work to clear out the obscurations in our view. It was not about seeking to attain something outside of ourselves other than who we are. Our work was to remove the blinders and open up the veils. They were also taught that the purpose of our entire existence was to grow our capacity to care, to cultivate what bodhicitta, the aspiration to alleviate the suffering of all sentient beings.

The habits of their culture were infused with the perfume of bodhicitta. Don't casually stomp on insects. Don't take for granted the animal life of the meat you eat. Don't see yourself, as a living being, superior to all other creatures, for it's likely you were them or will be them in a past or future life. All of existence is on a continuum; we are inseparable, and the laws of cause and effect, of karma, bounce us around that continuum from life to life, from hell realm to animal realm to god realm. Our human birth is but one of the possibilities we could have experienced, and being born in this realm is due to past actions, not to our superiority over others in this life. It's a precious birth, one where we're not so lost in suffering as in a hell realm, not so lost in pleasure as in a god realm, not so lost in thick-headedness or dullness as in the animal realm, and not so lost in an in-between bardo state. As dull as we seem, as deluded as we may be, as fragmented as our hearts and consciousness may feel, it is in this life, they believe, that we can most easily practice the dharma and clear the dust from our eyes. Our lives are precious, not to be squandered with frivolous pursuits or coarse actions. Meditate, say mantras, and keep building the imprints that lead to wisdom, in this life and the life to come.

I felt so much more myself and so much more at home here, with that aspiration as the foundation of the land, even if sometimes my hosts looked almost as if they were from a fantasy planet, wearing headdresses with big flaps sticking out like some kind of cosmic receiver, adorned with jewels that looked like they should have been the raiments of buddhas and bodhisattvas in the mythical realms. The Zanskari's clear eyes and kind hands, at times grasping my hand to make a point, made me feel more than connected—they made me feel a part of their world. A part of that flow of manifestation and life that ripples like waves, undulating on the surface of consciousness. They made me reflect on these things. Their warmheartedness gave room to these contemplations.

I was exhausted by my encounter with the trekkers and my dreams that night were vivid, confused, and full of Western attitudes that I felt uneasy with. I agonized in my dream about the gargantuan cost of higher education and of the pointlessness of returning to college to become a professional ... what? I kept insisting in my dream that I was only interested in being free and awake. But a shadowy figure insisted I needed to a skill that had a name.

When I woke up and tied my money belt on, I thought of the plane ticket inside, destination: Japan. Before I left America, among other subjects in University, I had studied Japanese. This time, when I found myself in Zanskar, was supposed to be—under the guidance of my advisor—spent studying the role of women in rural Japan. My unspoken plan had always been to learn enough Japanese so I could go to a Zendo and meditate. When I left America, I had no plans of going to India and had never even heard of Zanskar. The fact that I was here seemed either random or destiny. Instead of going straight to the Far East, I'd stopped in Thailand. There I'd heard about a magical place called Burma, where you could only get seven-day visas because of the tight-reined fascist regime. I visited and loved it and traveled on to Bangladesh and then Nepal. After my first ten-day retreat on the graduated path to awakening, my first trek, and months of quiet living on the far shore of Pokhara Lake, my Nepali visa ran out and I was required to take an exit trip to India. In the scorching heat of Varanasi in May, I'd fallen in love with the wild, chaotic, at times infuriating and cruel, profound land. The rest was history.

The next morning in Padum was lovely and sunny. There was a full spectrum rainbow painted auspiciously across the mountains. Krishna and I walked past the flour mills to stone huts built by the river for washing. We heated water on the kerosene stove, a luxury. It made the temperature bearable and felt so good to be clean. It was when we got back to the house, bright and refreshed, I did it. I lightened my load. I tore up my plane ticket to Japan. It was worthless to me now and holding onto it was just a psychological weight. Though it had cost what I could live on here for six months, the money was already gone. What was the value of that money anyway? Traveling to Japan would be going back into a technological world. I would end up searching for the simplicity and harmony of the Zen teachings among high-speed trains, microwave ovens, and supercomputers. That was someone else's dream, not my own, an abstraction I had built into a plan. The life in the mountains, working out my own salvation with diligence, as the Dhammapada advised, was exactly where I wanted to be. Three months after my twenty-first birthday, I was choosing a different fork in the crossroads. It seemed, really, to be the only one I could take.

Sometimes the choices we make feel like choiceless acts, decisions propelled by some inner momentum, some karmic continuum that has to unfold in that certain way. I may have thought I was choosing, but what I chose were the options that spoke the loudest to me. With the teachings on spiritual imprints from past lives, I could relate to my choices as a journey that began long before. I felt as much a follower in my own life as a trailblazer.

I thought of my parents and guilt flashed through me; they were always so disappointed when I didn't take the well-worn road and sudden changes made them nervous. They and I heard very different callings. To me, my changes of direction weren't sudden at all. When I peeled another layer off and saw the kernel of the matter, there wasn't really a choice, one way was obvious. How could I have known I'd end up in Zanskar before? It hadn't been clear yet. I had to uncover it, walking off the layers of my preconceived plans and culturally conditioned goals. The idea of going to Japan and finishing college made me feel more like one of the Zanskari mules following a fragrant turnip round and round the mill wheel. I didn't want to grind someone else's flour.

Lifting the veils of unquestioned expectations sometimes looks like straining forward and sometimes like letting go. For me, this was both. I was liberating myself from a role that was logical and set to yield some culturally permissible and ego-gratifying results: researching to advance women's studies, identifying cultural structures to create better communities, and acquiring an academic degree. For me, pursuing a university degree was like setting a match to the dry kindling of competitiveness, pride, and position, a socially respected— but not a soul-uplifting—end. The direction I chose instead, walking in my running shoes held together by string and cobbler's glue, was a response to the calling only I could hear, that small song of my soul.

It relieved me to be so far from a post office. I had no pressure to explain or justify my decision to anyone else. I just made it and continued. No one could see a sea change in direction but me. I felt infinitely lighter.

I no longer needed to hurry. I didn't need to meet a deadline. What was my real destination? What was the purpose of the path I had chosen? My needs were conditioned, not real in any other sense but relative. In America, I needed a college degree, a job, and nice clothes. Here, I felt more connected to a different need, one that I couldn't shake, one that compelled me to commit to going to the end of the search, to discover what made sense in Life, with a capital L. The real answer wasn't status or accomplishment, but the softness I saw in the Lamas' eyes. Their transparency went in and in and in, luminous, open, and still. In them, I saw no protective walls filtering out the light, no reaching off-balance for false gods of security or fame. From now on, I prayed to nothing in particular, I wanted to walk without false obligations and give everything to go as far as I possibly could in this life.

Moti had loaned me a copy of the 1920s travel log by A. Reeve and Kathleen Ann Heber called *Himalayan Tibet and Ladakh*. I spent the afternoon reading and sleeping. It was a gorgeous day, so light and free. There was a noisy and joyous wedding procession cutting through town. Life coming. Life going. The sky turned the deep blue of the ocean and the sun illuminated the entire mountain opposite my window. The government-issued house had the feel of colonial Britain, but I'd have still taken a Zanskari two-story home any time. When the snow came, it was much better to be above ground level.

In the afternoon, Hasan rushed in breathless to call us out and across town to the bank where a crowd of over one-hundred people had gathered. The mood was fiery. Muslims crowded to one side, shouting in loud, angry voices while the Buddhists drew together opposing them, the men discussing in quiet tones and some of the cheeky young girls calling out taunts. The Muslims wanted to build a new, large mosque and a graveyard on land that the Buddhists claimed belonged to them and which was an irreplaceable part of the area's limited grazing land. They had brought their case to the Hindu superintendent to mitigate. It was a serious matter and no decision would be reached for quite some time. The handful of Indian officials retreated from the doorway into a backroom with representatives from either side.

Padum contained about forty percent Muslims who were mostly brought in by the Indian government as laborers. I couldn't help but suspect that some of the government employees were working to antagonize and undermine the strong Zanskari loyalty. For centuries Bons, Muslims, and Buddhists had lived easily among one another in the valley. There was a flow and even delegation of trades between the groups. But with the centralized Indian government taking a stronger role in the area, the local cooperation was breaking down. National and international interreligious conflicts were now being brought into an area that was far removed from the origin of the discontent.

Prior to British rule in India, Padum had been the seat of one of the thrones of Zanskar. The locals tended to feel closer to the king of Zangla, but they afforded both palaces respect. Even though the kingdoms no longer exercised any significant control over the area, their rule and the Buddhist practices they aligned with were part of the backbone of the culture. Zanskar had long been an isolated and consolidated civilization, resistant to outside intrusion. With industrialization and a different level of trade and commodification, that was changing. The Muslims who had more recently moved into the area to assist with government building and roadwork were primarily of Sunni faith, and were far more assertive than the native Buddhists. They were uprooted, far from their home communities. The men had little that embedded them in the local community. Their customs came from a different land, lineage, and culture. The startling contrast between the customs was most visible in the children and women. Instead of laughing, dancing, and mischievously making contact the way Zanskari children did, the youngsters brought from outside the valley looked at me with unsmiling faces. The women turned away when I passed, walking the streets almost surreptitiously, as a wary cat does. Their culture restricts women's movement in public and around males who are not part of their immediate family. In this mixed marketplace, these women found themselves interacting more than was customary, and though necessary was still no doubt uncomfortable for them. I felt self-conscious under the disapproving eyes of their menfolk, who regarded a woman alone with a critical, mistrustful, or paternalistically protective response. They made me nervous. I had not felt this uncomfortable since I had left Srinagar. They never said or gestured disrespectfully, but I felt judged in their stares. I had been reading Sufi poetry and stories of the dervishes and mystical mendicants and appreciated the elevation of women under the Prophet Mohammed. I was in awe of the genteel Persian culture with its refined art, literature, medicine, and mathematics and the unparalleled Muslim hospitality that I experienced during my travels in India and in Egypt but my recent experience traveling as a woman alone in rapidly modernizing and changing Kashmir had jaded me.

Watching the conflict in front of me, the shouting and taunts, and the men getting heated, I hoped the magistrate would protect the local grazing grounds but I doubted that would be the outcome. I suspected the Indian government had much more to gain by supporting Kashmiri interests to help placate larger conflicts since Zanskar was officially under the control of Jammu and Kashmir, the Indian state populated by a Muslim majority, a state that lived in an uneasy truce with the Indian government, periodically boiling over in a push for its own independent rule.

The terrain where I'd been walking for the last few weeks had filled me with the peace and camaraderie of a powerfully close-knit and happy local culture. In these remote mountains, life hadn't changed much for the last fifteen hundred years. There was simplicity, harmony, sustainability in the villages. Most of all, I felt the release and relief of joy without conflict—neither interpersonal, regional, nor religious strife. In an afternoon, I had been transported from the harmonious Zanskari culture and the religion which valued cooperation, peaceful coexistence, and compassion to the geopolitics of the rising global powers of India and China, spiced with tensions with Pakistan. I had been plunged into the conflicts of the modern world. It was not exposure that I liked very much.

I was anxious to keep moving, though I also had some pre-travel anxiety making ants in my stomach. Before I went, however, Krishna wanted "Just one snap in a sari!" I went back inside and she dressed me. We posed dutifully, like sisters, freezing in our thin cotton outfits. I did not feel very graceful. When I had lived in Benares I would glide through the alleyways, my sari trailing behind me, feeling elegant and light as a butterfly, my back poker straight, my body lithe and full of a modest woman's pride. But here in Zanskar, I felt wide and bulky like a wooly zho, my body short, squat, and rounder in shape, my cheeks red-hued, chapped from wind and smoothed with butter rather than the even sun-touched bronze of the Indian plains.

Finally, goodbyes were said and I set out on the path once more, walking away from Padum. The sun, nestled in the turquoise sky, illuminated the whole mountain. The color and texture of the light were unmistakably Zanskar. It shone with a brilliance and intensity like nowhere else, strong but not harsh. The air was more clear than clear, as unobscured as a Buddha's vision. I loved this world.

Samsara, the circle of existences,
and nirvana, the state beyond it,
are not like geographical locations far from one
another.
They are two states of mind.

Samsara is a deviation from knowledge,
a distorted vision of reality
that makes the mind the slave of negative emotions,
while nirvana is a state of inner freedom,
free of any conceptual and emotional obstacles.

TENZIN GYATSO, THE XIV DALAI LAMA

(B. 1936)

Chapter Nine
Black Magic, Black Mind

It was so nice to be moving again, my muscles settled into their stride, my gait ate up the distance quickly. It was a good morning, a good life. I could feel the emptiness and freedom. I didn't feel alone. The environment was so rich with activity, color, texture, consciousness. And spirits.

The path, both physical and spiritual, presents all kinds of unexpected challenges. Without enough discrimination, experience, or guidance, a shadow could fall from nowhere and seem to veil the entire sun. I would have thought that the more I walked and ached with love for this simplicity, the more my mind would clear. Yet, again and again, I fell prey to darker thoughts and the isolation that accompanies them.

You could interpret these moods through all kinds of lenses—past trauma, *samskaras* ripening, wisps of depression, or spirits from another realm or dimension of consciousness. I began to think more about what I'd heard of the Bonpas, practitioners of the ancient Bon religion and its influence on life in the valley. Maybe it held an explanation for the ups and downs of my mood. I'd learned a little about the more esoteric aspects of this tradition from the reading I'd been able to do at Moti and Krishna's and from the conversations about enlightenment, tantra, and spiritual practice we had over the few days we spent together. Moti's stories and descriptions of unexplainable wild events raised the hair on my arms. He and his friends described powerful winds springing up from nowhere and circling just one house in a village, strange travelers that showed up at a village then vanished without a trace, a young woman going mad and speaking in tongues then returning to normal after a multi-day exorcism ritual. Some of the accounts were so eerily detailed they took shape again in the room as my friends recounted them. I'd also met longtime seekers who told me similar stories of spells and spirits and black magic practiced in this part of the world. It was hard to know what to make of it all but given how I'd been feeling all of a sudden, unhappy spirits seemed as good an explanation as any psychological one.

I wondered more about the Bon religion with its fascinating elements and contradictory descriptions. What was the real story? I hadn't met practitioners directly to be able to tell. There are several different views of its tradition, from what I understood it seems to have grown up organically in these mountains, a precursor of what is now the Tibetan Buddhist schools. Bon practice and its lineages are said to date back much closer to the time of Gautama the Buddha, emerging some 2,000 years ago. They were always dedicated to the alleviation of suffering, to the healing of the land and to the attainment of an awakened state of nonduality. In addition to nature spirit practices and divination, it had its own forms of meditation and a complex and serious path to enlightenment. Some say Bon practices formed the basis of Dzogchen, the Tibetan meditation path considered to be the highest teachings and the most direct route to liberation. Dzogchen meditation practices are renown to be the quickest way to penetrate dualistic views and perceive the ultimate nature of nondual reality. They are powerful and one must study for many years in a direct relationship with an accomplished master.

The original Bon temples and their line of yogis were highly revered by Tibetans, at least until the 800s, when an ambitious and selfish Tibetan king took the throne and sought to extend his power and rule. Under his reign, what was mutual respect degenerated into a widespread ransacking of the Bon temples in Zanskar. Sacred artifacts were removed from their original housings and installed in Nyingma temples. Some Bon temples were taken over wholesale and converted into Tibetan ones. What happened next is even harder to parse out. Bonpas say the Tibetan ruling class went on to sow rumors denigrating them and their religion, accusing them of being low level sorcerers and black magicians. They say that their highly evolved system of the meditative arts, with special secret powers including some still practiced by Nyingma lamas today—including transfiguration of a person into a light body, control of rain and storms, flying, vision into past and future lives and different realms of being, and ability to cast out spirits—was all derided as "black magic" by the Tibetans to justify their unscrupulous usurping of Bon spiritual power spots. They say the Tibetans intentionally disrupted their lineages and the oral practices handed down from generation to generation in order to elevate themselves.

With the respect that the Dalai Lama has extended to Bon practitioners, and the recognition of its exalted place as a foundational path of awakening in Tibet, attitudes are changing. Still, the rumor mill has a way of lingering regardless of historical accuracy, and this valley and its isolation and dramatic scenery is a perfect setting for sorcery, spells, and magic. The belief that Bon was a religion of manipulation through incantations is widespread. And the belief in sorcery and the remnants of unresolved spells is even more widespread. Children are threatened that sorcerers will find them if they misbehave, and misfortunes are often blamed on spells and witchcraft.

I certainly felt undercurrents that matched these descriptions. Whether spells were the result of unresolved negative actions, the spiteful wishes of a powerful but misaligned character that still lingered over a house, a cave, or a stream, or something far more esoteric like a being from one of the hell realms caught between two dimensions, there was no doubt that sometimes out of nowhere I'd feel a chill run through me. Cold but not just temperature, like a shadow that sucks out the life force. Externally, everything would look fine, but in my gut or in my bones, I'd feel a clammy foreboding, though I couldn't say what I was apprehensive about. Most times I'd keep moving, consciously gluing my eyes to the path, neither looking left nor right, running the smooth beads of my mala through my fingers, and reciting mantras aloud. Other times I'd recount the hindrances on the path to enlightenment and the six virtues. Sometimes the shadow traveled with me. I'd feel my mind get sucked into a whirlpool of doubt and the eerie branches in the dank forest of fear and uncertainty would snatch at my heart.

Two days north of Padum, heading back up on the second half of my journey, one of those spells cast its shadow over me. The path underfoot was clearly drawn and smooth, and the rocks shone in their beautiful palette of tawny beiges. I had been loving the way, filled with gratitude and wonder, then out of nowhere a chill descended. Walking along an irrigation ditch gurgling with grey glacial water, restless thoughts rose up. I saw a few dark marks of birds in the otherwise empty sky. I heard my feet crunch the sand. Was I mistaken? Was that an echo, a half step behind me? My pack grew heavier, caught in the drag of a wind current I couldn't otherwise feel. I looked around. No houses in sight. No other small figures in the distance. I was alone. But I didn't feel alone. Whatever was with me wasn't a presence I'd ever encountered before.

Committing to liberation in this life calls up all kinds of demons inner and outer. Whether it was purification working its way through me, the ripple of old hurts, karmas molting, or a test of my faith and resolve to see how committed I was to my quest for *rigpa* or pristine awareness, still I faltered. The more I struggled against my mind, the more enmeshed I became. Like a Chinese finger trap, when I wriggled and shimmied to extricate myself, the more tightly I was bound. I started to lose my inner way. On the spiritual path, when you wrestle with inner demons, you never get free. The trick is to keep your eyes on the goal. Bypass the mind, follow the time-honored instructions, and not worry about diagnosing the problem. Once you tarry in the quicksand of the hells of the mind, it becomes harder and harder to get out. Pretty soon I was stuck.

Unsure of what to do, I came upon a deserted gompa and sat down in the yard with a restless feeling. Big patches of stucco mud had fallen off the walls and some of the stones had loosened and rolled out of place. They lay in the courtyard like giant disembodied eyes, watching everything, guarding what was left of what had been a place of practice. There was a large mani wall on the far side of the courtyard still blowing mantras into the wind, and two once white stupas with their graceful pear-shaped curves. It felt a little safe because of the familiar symbols, the mantras carved on stone still blowing their blessings into the wind, and the echoes of the sacred chanting I imagined had gone on in the large hall at some time. It had a sense of protection and at the same time it was eerily empty, like I felt.

As I rested and tried to shake the cobwebs from my head, that familiar and unwelcome dirge of self-criticism and confusion settled over me like a fog. Not asleep but not quite awake, I daydreamed of senseless things, like where I would live, what messages I would leave on my answering machine, and what life would be like back at college. I thought about the friends I had grown up with, so many talented and creative people, yet I hadn't stayed in touch with a single one. Vignettes from the different sides of me during my adolescence came and went, they all seemed to contradict one another, leaving me with no center or ties to any one of those lives. How could a river ever parse out the waters of its tributaries? Yet in the stream running through my mind, that's what it seemed I was trying to do.

In my semi-sleep, the various life chapters that led to my resting here under this strange shadow with the clouds above me ran their narratives. It was like being in a movie theater with endless doors, catching snippets of one film then walking into another. Who was I? How did I get here? What made sense of it all? Was this whole journey crazy?

This was 1983 and I was neither early enough in the wave of East-meets-West to be a trailblazer, nor innocent enough to believe in the dawning revolution of love and light on a mass scale. Coming of age in the seventies, characteristically of my generation, I felt jaded, mistrustful, and suspicious. My friends and I felt duped by the lies of Watergate, cynical from our country's failure to eradicate racism, and dejected by our government's refusal to end the unconscionable violence in Viet Nam. "Question Authority" was the most popular bumper sticker of those years.

I had a women's liberation lens, too, that angry late second wave of feminism, bent on proving that anything men could do we could do better. It was me against the world, going wherever, whenever, often afraid, always pretending not to be.

I was marked by the sixties, still loving the melodic harmonies of *Traffic* but more immersed in the fantastical and distant epics of *Genesis*. I spent most of my high school days in the park behind the school, sitting in the grass, watching the trees, experimenting a little with consciousness expanding psychedelics, not looking for oblivion but looking for clues. We read Carlos Castaneda and Tolkien.

At night I trudged off to an alternative Hebrew High School, where for five years I met thrice weekly with four other girls, and we talked in Hebrew and explored *Pirke Avot* ethics and Biblical and Diaspora history, re-interpreting old texts and experiencing afresh historical indignities, searching for a moral compass we could actually use. Late night, I curled up over my journals, writing longhand poetry, smithing feelings into words into poems. I bucked social norms and men who lorded power and searched for the wise people. Like most adolescents of my generation, I tossed and turned, grasping for a type of love that didn't seem to exist anymore in our world.

The seventies were a desolate time but there were books. Richard Hittleman's *28 Day Guide to Yoga,* with his powerful transmission of a serious spiritual life camouflaged by his instructions on how to flatten your tummy. He was a student of the great Ramana Maharshi in the 1940s, and inspired me to spend a year in studying the nondual teachings of Advaita Vedanta, in Rishikesh at Sivananda Ashram. Swami Brahmananda was said to be one of the great living masters on the classical text *Yoga Vasishta* and he held class in his little monk's kutir at five in the morning.

The seeds we sow when we are young lead us places. Yogananda's *Autobiography of a Yogi* encouraged me to seek the great mystics and Ram Dass' *Be Here Now*, the Bible for seekers like me, gave me a sense that something extraordinary was possible. Spiritual books were lights in the tunnel of my adolescence. Their descriptions gave me a way to question and they encouraged me to feed that stirring inside, compelling me to not just untie the knots of my angst but to search for more.

Somehow, all those influences and choices led me to this abandoned temple. I sat up and lit a fire, boiling some tea, with extra sugar and powdered milk to calm my nerves. I ate a few stale Indian *Parle* biscuits, their vanilla smell brought a weak smile to my face. I could find my way through this. I knew a little bit more about the obstacles on the path to realization and a little bit more about the demons of doubt and fear than I used to. I knew a little more about the power of intention and commitment. And I knew a little about bad spirits and the wiliness of Mara.

Still, a little is not really enough to navigate the storms of mind alone when they come. The Tantric texts say you can transform anything, even the worst poison, into nectar once you discern the ultimate emptiness of all things. In the highest tantric practices, they say don't avoid anything, whatever arises, follow it all the way to penetrate the nature of absolutely all things. That path wasn't really for me. I was definitely trying to avoid these dark states of mind, any way I could.

The chai picked me up. The caffeine, sweet and warm filled me. Preparing and drinking, moment-to-moment actions gave me sense that there was something I could do. I wasn't empty-handed. I was on a mission, and I could keep going. I washed out my cooking pot with ash and sand, packed it away.

I stood up and surveyed my options. I wanted to cover ground and have some sense of progress. This state of mind was the harshest I'd experienced since I'd entered the valley. I was confident it would shift, everything eventually does. I would continue the single thing I knew I could do. Keep walking.

It looked like I could cut straight across the valley floor and get to the fold at the next mountain foot. I set out across the sea of stones. The greys of the rocks were surreal but also warm. The smoked sky was not dingy or sad but surreal and impenetrable like my feelings. Some hours later, I found an empty herder's hut to stay in for the night. These were huts used communally by shepherds who would bring their yaks and goats to the area for the day or longer. Often times children as young as eight or twelve would come with the animals so their parents could work the more physically demanding jobs in the fields. This one hadn't been used recently but it wasn't abandoned and I could imagine a couple of Zanskari children, throwing rocks, making piercing whistles with blades of grass between their fingers, singing, and leaping around. They'd hug and cuddle the young yaks and bleating lambs.

While the shepherds' huts were solitary, away from the villages so the herds wouldn't trample the fields and eat the next winter's grains, they weren't lonely. Like most of the huts, this one had three walls and an open space for entrance. It was a tight space with no roof but it would work for the night. I settled in, built a small fire pit and lit a fire for a little company and to heat tea and some soy nuggets with curry spices. I'd run out of cooking oil and forgotten to see if I could buy some yak butter from the last village I'd passed through so the sauce was a little thin and bitter. Not my most gourmet of meals but, like the hut, it worked for the moment. I felt fortunate to be fed, warm, and protected against the elements. I thought about the happy Zanskaris. They were so steeped, like strong tea, in the teachings on inherent Buddha nature, impermanence, and karma, you couldn't separate the amber color from the water, or the wellbeing from the people. They filled me with longing and admiration.

Even though I felt so foreign, I was learning from

them. Breathing the air in this valley, I inhaled nutrients for my soul. Rich, loamy, fertile. Still, my ground was going to need a lot more restoration, it was more like a corner scrap metal junkyard in a rougher section of a city. It was going to take a lot of clearing out and reclamation first.

Not surprisingly, my mind was still unsettled and as much as I was holding myself together, it still felt a bit spooky to be alone. I took comfort from the emerald stars peeking through the patchy night clouds. The smell of stone, dirt floor, baked mud and straw stucco felt familiar and safe. Cliff swallows swooped over me in graceful arcs of wild choreography and there were animal calls somewhere in the distance. I slipped into sleep, giving my conscious mind a rest and allowing the tangles of my soul to unravel on their own.

I hoped that the clouds would pass by morning but the journey to clarity doesn't usually work that smoothly. The morning light still didn't dispel my mental shadows. A stale restlessness itched in my bones. Even in the middle of an empty shepherd's hut I was irritable with everyone, including myself. I had been heading towards the renowned Karsha Gompa, one of the most vibrant monasteries in the valley. The thought of trekking inland to visit and pay respects, which normally would lift my spirits and remind me of what I was on this quest for, filled me with annoyance.

Karsha was the largest monastery in the area, with something like one-hundred and fifty monks and a number of highly esteemed lamas. A Gelug monastery, built in the tenth or eleventh century, it held the echoes of countless hours of focused prayer and practice. Usually, I'd love to sit there, and drink in the presence, maybe be fortunate enough to meditate during a special puja. But my sullenness cast a negative light on everything. A few extra hours trudge to see a dark, archaic, male-dominated temple? What could I possible learn when I knew so little about what they were really chanting? Was I truly a spiritual seeker or just filled with ego, arrogance, and self-delusion? Doubt of one's own sincerity is one of the most difficult doubts to navigate. With its oily voice of reason and logic, it slicks the grooves of the mind and next thing you know the machinery of negativity has picked up pace and is chugging along, away from wholeness.

I decided not to visit the monastery. And I was determined to walk right through this mood. Walking helped me think more positively or not think at all, which at times like these was often the best. My legs took in the distance, one stride after another. Physically, at least, I was moving, even if the record needle kept skipping back to the same track. I had to backtrack to the path to get over the bridge. My shortcut had led me straight to a raging river with no place to cross. It felt metaphoric. I walked back the couple hours to the trail that was going to lead me where I intended to go. Rebellion on the path doesn't really work out. It's not the right energy to follow. Even though my shortcut hadn't saved any time it appeared I was passing through something and the lessons were helpful. Trekking is a physical metaphor for spiritual development.

I stopped and sat on a boulder, pulled out my map and looked at the ridges and the dotted line of the footpath. I figured out how far I thought I could make it if I walked steadily through the rest of the day. I translated the two-dimensional contours into what I thought it would feel like to my legs and settled on the next marker as I made my way north to Zangla, the village where the King of Zanskar lived. Oriented and with a plan now, I folded the old army map, stained and softened with wear, hoisted my pack back on my shoulders, and set off, thinking about what was propelling me forward and all I was learning.

The foundational tenets of the Buddha dharma have always made sense to me, the repudiation of the caste system, women's freedom, respect and love of other beings, valuing direct experience, and raising the quality of consciousness and, from there, the quality of life. While I imagined that, throughout history, there had been both greater and less well-motivated Buddhist adepts and monastics, it wasn't the same tenor as the blood and vengeance of the Old Testament, the crusades and colonization in the name of the New, or the conquest at the hands of the Ottomans. It was not a religion red in tooth and claw. As a system of self-realization, it was the one of ones I found most resonance with.

But I did not come to Zanskar to cast off one set of cultural rules for another. I wanted to unpeel the veils that clouded my heart and mind and limited what was possible. That dust of ignorance on the mirror of the self, tempered the good that I could bring into the world. Our world needs transformation, and for that, we needed individuals who didn't just see differently, but who were different.

And so I walked. Walked through my mind. Walked through the ignorant and deluded emotions that overtook me. Walked through my selfishness. Walked through my judgments, walked through my fears. It was my *tapas,* my spiritual practice or austerity. I intended this walking to help polish the rough edges of myself.

As hard as my mental state was, I felt held in the midst of these massive and majestic mountains. So high up, I could feel the curve of the earth and its roundness. I could feel the energy, the current of the whole. I've never wanted to go to the moon, but I imagine this was the feeling Edgar Mitchell had when he looked back at the exquisite blue marble of the earth from above. We're not separate in our little villages or big cities. Our waters flow from one territory to the next. The birds soar across an undifferentiated sky. There is a recognition of Being that is unbounded. I could feel it. Somehow, I already knew it but had forgotten somewhere along the way of birth and life's activity.

My bones were at home within this pristine awareness of a living current of knowing, one that encompassed far more than the world of my mind, with all its inconsequential, though painful, negativity. I couldn't quite touch what I was sensing but the refuge I was finding felt so deep and familiar. If I could hug the mountains I would, wrap my arms around them and merge into their bosom and know—in that beyond-the-mind sense of knowing—the living ground of goodness and knowledge, that innermost nature of all that is.

While at the same time, I also still felt separate from my goal, I was not, and I knew, in a way I couldn't describe, that that inherent goodness was tangible, more real than real. It was filled with a zest for life and its essence was love.

The Zanskaris, from the youngest roly-poly toddlers to the vivacious teenagers, to the happy parents, to the contented elders, knew the incense of this higher consciousness. Like the earthy fragrance of the yak is inseparable from the woven coats they wear, this scent of nonseparation is inseparable from all their ways of being. Trust, faith, and devotion were the unspoken currency of their relationships.

Here, in spite of the shadows of my mind, I moved and breathed amidst an ethos that valued life. Their teachings saw all beings as consciousness, as empty of independent existence or isolation, as one. Here, non-separation was not a cold nihilism. It was not the dark corners of the mind. Its woof and shuttle wove a tapestry of compassion so vast it shattered the limits of the mind. Bodhicitta, that exultant desire and vow to uplift all sentient beings—from the scariest demons to the most irresistible gods—and free them from the endless cycle of suffering, from the repetitive trauma of birth, death, and rebirth, through various stages of ignorance and delusion, guided actions and our relationship to our own mind. As the teachings go, cultivating bodhicitta, caring that much, was the best antidote to dark states of mind.

I had first heard these teachings at a hillside monastery in Nepal a year earlier. I had spent time sitting silently reflecting on the nature of a love that was more gentleness and nonseparation than the bridge of emotion I thought of as connection or intimacy. It was not love as in me-and-you or an action to be done, but rather an embodiment, an integration. Awakening to bodhicitta makes that kindness a part of one's existence, as our blood flows through the uncountable capillaries in our bodies. Awakening to that care becomes the oxygen of existence itself. I could feel how it could infuse life with purpose and direction, and how it could reveal a very different way of being, something radical, an enormous, all-encompassing, nonsticky love.

That kind of love doesn't have a name in English. Our worldview is one of dualism, of this and that, of subject and object, of you and me. It makes that kind of care feel daunting, exhausting, self-denying. Emptiness and bodhicitta were inseparable. When we see ourselves as separate, we see our resources as limited and the idea of uplifting all beings through their endless cycles of birth and death and evolution to a full awakening feels like a crushing weight. You also can't separate bodhicitta from an understanding of the cyclical nature of existence or how that relates to the consciousness that permeates all things and recognizes that our particular form is transient, an outline on a frosty window that blurs and melts in the sun.

I remember as a small child, squatting down on my chubby toddler's legs, before I could speak, to peer into the black faces of the purple pansies that lined the walk to our apartment. I would talk to them, loving them, and murmuring to them, telling the ones with sad faces not to be sad. When I got older, I was no longer able to have those conversations, but like many teens, I wanted to change the world. When I looked at the war, greed, and environmental degradation, the obviousness of the need for a better way and of my insufficiency overwhelmed me. That's when I consciously made the decision to pursue a wisdom that would be able to actually do something at a level beyond my small self.

I hadn't been introduced to the Mahayana way of seeing the world yet and the weight of suffering weighed heavy on me. Bodhicitta was that different way of seeing. It made everything possible, not in spite of—but because of—the enormity of its aspiration. It brought the Lamas joy. The more deeply they cultivated bodhicitta, the more radiant they became. Their skin glowed, their eyes sparkled, and they moved with timelessness and weightlessness whether they were praying, chanting mantras, or walking through a crowded street market, joking with the vendors.

Bodhicitta is a way of being the Zanskaris live by. I'd never imagined it was possible for real, but I felt it here in the Copper Valley. Here was a key that fit, that could unlock the mountain of my angst. And so I kept walking, through the clouds of my mind's darkness.

*On seeing or hearing about a dear person
being happy, cheerful, and glad,
unselfish joy can be aroused by thinking:
"This person is indeed happy! How good, how
excellent!"*

*How does a practitioner live with their heart
filled with gladness?
Just as they would be glad
on seeing a dear and beloved person,
so they pervade all beings with gladness.*

BUDDHAGHOSA
(5TH CENTURY CE)

Chapter Ten
Women, Men & the Scariest Bridge

Crossing the bridge brought me to a more beautiful side of the valley. The rocks were dramatic, so many different lines of color, painted by epochs of history, shaded with changing minerals and pre-historic plant matter baked into their essential elements. As huge as they were, I wanted to wipe my hand across the sediment lines, to read the braille of the earth's evolution. The simplest ingredients—earth, sky, light, and water—made infinite designs, one more beautiful than the other. It felt like the valley of the Gods, and I felt small and humbled to be there. I found a yak hut without a roof just past Karsha and boiled a mean tea over a fire fueled by dried yak and sheep dung and pricker weeds. It was a lot of work to get the water boiled at that elevation.

For no reason, I started to feel nervous; the thought crossed my mind that I was completely alone, no one who knew me or would protect me if someone with ill intention would come. I jumped when a few cliff swallows swooped suddenly down over me. It was just my memories playing tricks on me. I never worried in Zanskar, which was so unlike my experience growing up in America. I never felt that irrational violence and anger that was becoming more and more the norm in my birth country. I grew up in the generation of the first Milkcarton kids, of warnings not to talk to strangers. Here, I was the one who felt rough. The people I met were so self-contained and self-assured, I always felt safe with them. I never felt they wanted to take anything from me or harm me in any way. They were always giving, smiling, offering endless tea and tsampa. They showed me care, not because of who I was but because I was a sentient being like all others, towards whom care was extended.

I thought about the teachings I'd learned, that hadn't made sense to me at the time. In Tibetan Buddhism they talk about seeing each sentient being as if they were your mother, because given all our countless karmic rebirths, they had been in a previous incarnation. Your mother gives her body and gives you life, and you repay that kindness with your gestures of compassion, never causing harm, always extending care. I had a more postmodern and ambivalent relationship with my parents. But here, the sense of how existence emerges and subsides is woven into the fabric of life.

I never made it to Karsha Gompa, but the town of Karsha was beautiful, well-populated with a jaunty vibrant air. As I walked through the town, a couple of women called to me from a four-story rooftop, gesticulating wildly and insistently. The village was a maze hanging on the cliff, large and surreal. They sent a young girl down to fetch me. When I crawled up the last few stairs I walked in on a gala. It was women's social hour, and a festive one at that. It was late afternoon and the room was packed with women of all ages, along with a passel of toddlers, and infants. They had been drinking their local barley beer for quite some time and were full of bawdiness and laughter. They poured me a cup, and another, and a third. Spooning chang into their babies' mouths, their breasts hanging out of open vests, they drank and fed the infants, sometimes exchanging babies with one another to nurse. With a large tambourine, some drums, and bells, they danced and sang in the small space with their shirts half off, sometimes laughing so hard at the verses they crumpled to the floor. They grabbed me and, after too much chang, I found myself dancing Zanskari folk dances too.

When they noticed the sky darkening, they collected their ladles and cups one by one, tucked them into the folds of their vests, buttoned up, and made their way home, tottering slightly, to tend to the animals and prepare dinner. They knew how to enjoy life. Such cheekiness and raucous abandon, confidence,and contentedness they had in their lives. I also made my way. I had seen a yak hut a little further along the path and in no time I was there. I laid out my pad and bedroll, grateful. On any given day, I could pass through wildly different chapters and states of mind. I fell asleep looking up through the open roof at the brilliant stars. My dreams, if there were any, were peaceful.

I woke to a cloudless morning. The air and light were uniquely clear. I made tea and little rotis, some dense flatbreads I could eat now and nibble on throughout the day. I still had a few peanuts and Ladakhi apricots that I cooked into the rotis, it made them a little more interesting and would keep me going all day. My life and diet had become very simple. Porridge, rotis, soy nuggets, rice, dal, and mostly, of course, tsampa with butter and salt.

The way north took me through a long, flat valley. It was dry and hot, desert-like. The sun burned through the rarified air, I can see why the Zanskaris put thick butter on their cheeks to protect them from sunburn and wind chaffing. Some light clouds came over the midmorning sky which made it easier to trek. Roses bloomed in tiny pink splashes and I noticed many flies. I hadn't paid attention, or maybe there hadn't been flies in the areas I'd walked through.

Funny, the things you become aware of when you are at ground level, moving at the pace your body can take you. The world of motorcars seemed so far away. I realized that though I'd seen a few army jeeps in the barracks in Padum, I hadn't heard anything mechanized, not a car or even a plane, since I disembarked from the bus three weeks earlier. I loved it here. The mountains were no longer the greenish tint of Padum but a variety of purples, lavender and periwinkle, plum and vintage violet. Much of the way was like being in the desert or on the beach. My feet sank into thick, slippery sand that made the going slow. In other sections, sharp, loose scree frosted the path, which dropped off sharply on one side into the river. These sections required concentration and invoked fear. I let go of my contemplation and focused.

I arrived a little before midday at Pishu, a fair-sized town. I sat beside two men soaking spun wool in large wooden buckets of water, and dyeing cloth in wine-colored juice. The woven folds were dense and heavy, it took a long time for the dye to penetrate. They used wood paddles to lift the lengths and turn them, allowing the color to bleed in evenly throughout. They sang as they worked. Everything seemed to have a song in Zanskar. Songs for the weeding, songs for bringing the goats in, songs for carrying water, songs to help the children fall asleep. I couldn't catch the words but I hummed with them, and they doubled over in laughter.

Soon, a household of six brothers invited me in for tea and tsampa. They were kind and curious, proud to tell me that two of the brothers were married to the same wife. Zanskari men are an interesting mix, they are neither traditionally masculine in the way Westerners describe masculinity, which usually means some degree of machismo, nor are they effeminate. They are strong and virile and soft and kind. They are handsome with radiant skin and clear eyes. Their hair is usually in two long thin braids which they tie up over their heads and their turquoise earrings are less like an adornment and more like a link or bridge to the land they blend in with. Zanskari men work hard and laugh often, they sing, rock babies, tell stories, and pray and bow before holy objects. They fall into quiet devotion as they pass a mani wall or circumambulate around a small stupa that holds relics of a great lama. And they race each other on horseback, tease and jest, and are sensitive to the group around them. The men talked among themselves and some to me. One invited me to stay the night. It was tempting to rest here, but I thanked them and told them I would continue on. I explained I was heading to the palace of the King of Zanskar. One brother cautioned me, "The wind picks up in the late afternoon, it will make your crossing dangerous. You must go quickly now or stay in our village tonight."

I took my leave and walked downstairs, lifted my pack on my shoulders, it felt lighter after the company of six strong men, who were so kind. I was excited to move because across the river was the renowned King of Zanskar and the palace of Zangla. I headed towards the bridge which was still out of my sight, about an hour in the distance. On the way I met a Danish couple, the first travelers I'd seen since Padum. They were well-equipped and good-spirited. They walked with two horses carrying ropes and other climbing gear and two guides. They had climbed some of the highest peaks in the world, some 7,000 meters or so, and they treated me to sweet milk tea and European crackers. We were joined by a Swiss fellow, Roger, who, like me was walking alone towards Lamayuru. For whatever reason, this little section of the path was a meeting point. It was almost like we had all materialized out of nowhere and happened to meet at the same spot at the same time. Surrounded by such a vast expanse of stone and sky, it sometimes seemed odd for us, such small creatures, to connect almost like we were mirages or manifestations of someone else's narrative. But we at least seemed real to me, not a wrinkle in consciousness, and I enjoyed seeing them.

Roger and I were heading the same direction and we agreed to walk together to Zangla. He was a reserved Genevan. Lanky and tall, with a nylon skiing cap and a mountaineering jacket that hung a little loose on his narrow frame. We seemed about the same age, give or take, though he seemed so much more directed than I. He told me he was a computer analyst, and I felt his cultural punctuality and clean-cut Protestant background. As he tightened the straps of his pack, I noticed his fingers, long and pale. My hands felt dirty and stubby in comparison. It was nice to have company for a ways. I felt bored of my own thoughts and he was soft-spoken and reserved which made for interesting but sparse conversation. He had much more mountaineering experience, skiing from the time he was three and hiking and climbing in the alps for as long as he could remember. He was athletic in a mountaineering sort of way, agile and comfortable in his frame, his long legs ate up the distance easily. He'd step, then spring forward, an interesting combination of effort and the extra propulsion that gave his gait a smooth and efficient rhythm.

I was a little envious of the protection his sturdy boots gave. My pink Nike running shoes, much as I loved them, weren't really made to go hundreds of miles in the mountains, and these had already carried me around Langtang in Nepal, up and down through villages in Himachal Pradesh and Kashmir and they were giving out. I kept the sole and uppers of my left shoe together with string, the Srinagar cobblers' glue had long since given way. I could feel the edges of the sharp stones as I trampled forward. Roger had been in India just a month and knew he was heading back to his country and his job in another month. Truth be told, much as it was nice to have a companion, I felt a little resentful of his presence. He reminded that I was not nearly as assimilated into the local culture as I liked to think, nor was I the pioneering romantic explorer I sometimes imagined myself to be.

I hadn't understood what the concern about the bridge was for. The valley seemed similar to the terrain I had covered the past few days and I encountered no difficulties with excessive winds. But I soon found out. To reach the palace of Zangla one must cross the river, which was accomplished only by the brave and strong-hearted. I had arrived at my first rope bridge. It was over 200-feet long, constructed not with actual rope, but with small twigs plaited together. The twigs were quite short in length, none of them over half-a-foot long, and braided four together into a thick rope. Several of these ropes were laid side by side to make the base which, upon closer inspection, was fortunately reinforced with steel cable. A thinner strand on either side served as a handrail. But these seemed less for use and more for show, giving only the illusion of something to steady your hands on. The wind tossed the flimsy structure about and the thick, ice-green water hissed and churned hundreds of feet below. I felt my stomach drop and had to breathe deeply to steady my shaking hands.

I had a mild fear of heights, something that only took over when I had a little too much time to think about the surroundings. Vertigo is an unique feeling, mesmerizing. It creates waves of nausea and is oddly compelling. I looked at the bridge and the couple hundred-foot drop to the water. I looked back at the twigs and saw how many of them were cracked. Though it was good I wasn't on my own for this, I was also mortified that on my first day trekking with an Alpine hiker, I would be shown to be clumsy, inexperienced, and weak. I wasn't sure which got me more, my fear or my embarrassment. The water swirled. Fear was definitely stronger. Roger went first. He was cautious but steady. I waited for him to safely cross, only learning later that it helps stabilize the bridge if there's more weight on it at the same time. I had no choice, I had to take the next step. I couldn't turn back at this point. I closed my eyes and said some prayers. That calmed me. I felt a wash of safety run through me.

I took hold of the handrails, such as they were, and stepped forward, careful to keep my feet turned out so the cable was secure under the arch of my foot. My mind ran through what I would do if I slipped, how to grasp the rails and wrap my legs around the cable. The handrails sank with my weight, so they were below thigh height. They must have been attached to the bottom of the bridge somewhere. There wasn't time to think all that through. Just one foot in front of the other. Step by step. As I moved further from the bank out over the water, I felt a cold wind. It was fresh and sharp, not enough to throw me off track but enough to grasp, in a visceral way, what my host had meant about the late afternoon wind. Step by step. My muscles were shaking. My hands were clenched so tight, I was squeezing my flesh into the braided rope so it and I would stay together no matter what. Breathe, I told myself. Muscles react better with oxygen. Nerves settle with inhalation and exhalation. My chest hurt from the pounding of my heart. My throat was tight. I was never one to love roller coasters or thrill rides. I loved adventure but not danger for danger's sake. I was willing to experience danger for the sake of a greater goal though. So here I was. I passed the middle of the bridge where the wind was strongest. Roger stood in between the posts on the other side, pack off, ready to come if he needed to. I smiled. I was going to make it. One foot then the other. The last twenty feet were easier but still every step took full attention, full concentration, and trust. In the mountains, faced by danger, trust and surrender help as much as strength and skill. I let go, not my focus, but of my desire to control, of that part of the mind that holds too tightly and tries to own what it cannot. Suddenly, my mind cleared and calmed, like another mind altogether. Everything opened up. The sky. The river. The rope. My weight. Everything felt connected in one shimmering net of energy. Something flashed, "There is nowhere to fall if everything is one." Next thing I knew, I heard the scratch as my foot touched the gravel of the far bank. I had made it.

Roger and I whooped our victory and celebration, startling some cliff swallows. We each took a few photos, to memorialize the moment, also because I didn't think I would believe myself if I described crossing a rope-twig bridge to anyone. We took out our maps, looked at roughly where we intended to reach and find a place to camp before the sun went down, and walked on in a friendly silence, listening to the sound of our shoes on the stones, the call of the wind, and the murmur of the mountains. It was good to be alive. It was a blessing to be in this special valley.

Yawning Mouth, the author at the base of the Drang Drung glacier, Zanskar.

Happy Village, Jildo, Zanskar.

Hospitality at Mohammed's, visiting with a Dard family along the Suru River, Zanskar.

Rock, Stupa, Village, approaching one of the towns along the path.

The World-traveling Rinpoche, A Lama with his attendants camped near Pensi La, Zanskar.

Wise & Light of Spirit, A Zanskari woman spins wool and dries yak cheese in the courtyard sun.

Making Torma Offerings, a resident monk at Rangdom Gompa prepares for a prayer service.

Everyone Gets Teased, two sisters weeding.

Ladling Tea at the Party, a woman manages boiling salt butter tea while nursing in an afternoon women's gathering.

A Sea of Black Rocks, unusual geological formations on the roof of the world, Zanskar.

Sisters Meeting, Zanskari travelers on the road outside of Padum, Zanskar.

Women Will Be Women, women picking spinach-like greens for dinner, Zanskar.

Crossing a Rope Bridge, braided twigs form a 220 ft. makeshift bridge over the ice-cold river near Zangla.

A Snap in a Sari, Krishna & the author dress for a photo. Padum, Zanskar.

Balanced on Scree, fellow traveler, Roger from Switzerland, 4,000 meters above sea level.

Monastery Nestled in the Mountainside, Lingshet Gompa (circled), walking path (arrows).

Tsampa for Breakfast, Tsampa for Tea, the temple storekeeper feeds villagers during the annual puja, Lingshet Gompa, Zanskar.

Dancing, Drinking, Celebration!, folk dances in the twilight under the great cliffs, Lingshet, Zanskar.

Be Happy!, a monk keeps his head cool and he walks with the author towards Lamayuru, Zanskar.

A Chorten Marks the Way, Singi La, 5060 meters, Zanskar.

It's Festival Time, villagers celebrating after the puja ends, Lingshet Monastery, Zanskar

Blessings in the Wind, hand carved Buddhas and mantras sanctify the way, a mani wall, Zanskar.

Genuine renunciation involves determination
to overcome ignorance, our real enemy.
This determination begins to manifest
when we realize that we are slaves of mental
confusion
and that there is little space for true happiness in our
lives. When this feeling becomes unbearable,
our only preoccupation is to get free.

TENZIN GYATSO, THE XIV DALAI LAMA
(B. 1936)

Chapter Eleven
Red Lipstick & A King's Welcome

Roger and I had fallen into an easy rhythm. We found enough material for a fire though it was nice to know he carried a propane stove with him. Dinner was simple bullion, soy nuggets, and dried noodles. And there were some Swiss chocolate treats to round off the night. Roger slept in his tent, I under the stars.

When I woke the next morning, I was unexpectedly excited. I was about to go to a real living palace, with a ruling king. Part of me still thought kings and palaces were the stuff from the fairytales I'd loved as a child. Yet here I was heading to a palace. I'd heard from other travelers in the Kangra Valley that the King was used to receiving visitors and was very hospitable. It was not like I could have called in advance to check if it was ok to come, or even find out if he was in residence, but I had been reassured by that pair of meditators that he was pretty much always there and was more than a titular head. He was a deep practitioner too. The mental picture built up my sense of expectation. This royal lineage was in part responsible for the long-term stability of the valley and the fact that the King was known to be a sincere practitioner of the Dharma, was one of the details that made me most eager to meet him.

By noon, we'd already walked for almost six hours.

It was quiet and very green. The summer crops were growing well and the fields felt alive with energy. The sheep and yaks had all been sent to higher pastures while the meadows ripened. The valley opened like a massive bouquet. Hundreds of flowers ringed the fields and an endless stretch of edelweiss shone in the sun. Sweet-smelling grasses and dal were in bloom. Butterfly pink flowers, clover, Queen Anne's Lace, and sky-blue poppies dotted the fields. I felt strong and in my stride. Walking in the mountains was as much a play of the mind as the body. Sometimes I felt like I was growing sturdier and thicker and sometimes I felt like I was shrinking into a fraction of myself, a pebble in the scree of the mountain debris. Today was a strong day and my legs swallowed the distance, heading forward.

The valley opened up; I could barely sense the walls of rock on both sides. The floor had changed in color and texture, now made up of a collection of sandy brown rocks and rectangular grey boulders. Throughout the day, the land dressed in different shapes and hues, telling a geological story in subtle shifts that revealed the million-year movements of minerals, heat, ice, and force. Taking the landscape in, I felt like I was time-traveling across the eons.

Then, something caught my eye. Could it be? Was I lucid dreaming an old western movie or some avant-garde Australian comedy? I saw a figure in the distance heading towards me on horseback. The first thing that registered was a streak of bright red lipstick, a red gash in a beige landscape. Like modern art, one mark drew the eye magnetically, filled with allure and mystery. Soon, a whole party came into view, about ten Zanskaris on ponies with saddlebags and gear, an odd entourage moving towards me. As they drew close, I could see the red-lipped woman at the front more clearly. And, to my surprise, at the front of her saddle rode a Lhasa Apso, his little dog head raised, drinking in the wind.

When we came within shouting distance, she called "Bonjour! Bonjour!" and waved enthusiastically. When she drew closer, she remained, in an inimitable French way, just as striking. She sat comfortably on her horse, with bright colored floral trousers, a scarf to match and an air of femininity that her culture has raised to a fine art. She must have been in her late fifties, as full of *joie de vivre* as anyone I'd ever met. Hailing from the South of France, she came every few years to visit with the King of Zanskar. It was not the dharma or the mountains that drew her here, she was a cynophile, a lover of dogs. Her passion took her, on her own, to this most remote of places, crossing for days on horseback and sleeping in tents, to meet the most august Lhasa Apso breeder in the world. Every year she bought at least one of his dogs to bring back to Europe. Apsos are loved by the Tibetans. In Dharamsala, I'd sometimes see monks outside their mountain huts reading texts, their dog warming their laps. Some recluses would even take them on long retreats in the mountains, feeling a connection, they'd say, from a previous birth. Other monks would hold them during prayers and pujas, believing that hearing the sacred mantras would leave auspicious impressions on the dog's consciousness and guide them to a better rebirth in a human or Buddha realm. I didn't know if this woman knew much about any of that, but it seemed a kind of karmic ripening and comic relief that we crossed paths that day. Whoever she was, her presence and mystery trailed behind her like a French perfume in an empty room, a hint but nothing more.

Soon after this encounter, we reached the palace. The royal lineage dated back one thousand years. The older palace, some nine-hundred years old, sat dramatically atop a cliff hundreds of meters above the village on an isolated, rocky outcrop serenaded by the biting wind and stalking eagles. The king's current abode was more modest and manageable. Built about 700 years ago, it was an extra-large and well-kept Zanskari house overlooking the fields and willow trees of the village. The biggest difference between the king's house and a common villager's was that his roof was finished with a neat and painted trim and was not lined with the ring of brush that looked so much like a punk haircut.

The king himself was a lovely and unassuming old man. Before we'd arrived I had drawn fantasies of him in my mind based on the kings that inhabited the worlds of Hans

Christian Anderson or the Brothers Grimm. But the jewels, brocades, carvings, tapestries, and magic brought to life in those stories missed this royal reality by a great many leagues. The king welcomed us into his study where he sat on Tibetan carpets in front of a low table. Among the thangkas decorating the walls hung several photos of His Holiness the Dalai Lama, a poster of Mahatma Gandhi, and three postcards of Japanese temples, sent to him by appreciative visitors. He spoke affectionately to his nine yappy Apsos and Tibetan Pekingese dogs. He treated them like children or wise old men and only shooed them out when they became too frisky and attention-seeking as he talked with us.

We talked with the king over butter tea about his son who was due to arrive the next day. Since the Indian government had set up rule in the area, the king had been divested of his authority and duties, although local people still liked and respected him as a ruler. His son had received an appointment by the Indian government and spent much of his time traveling throughout the valley surveying land, judging where bridges needed to be built and then reporting his findings in Leh, Kargil, and Srinagar. He had been educated at Banaras Hindu University and was no doubt a clever fellow, but the Kashmiri government gave little opportunity for the local Zanskaris to apply their talent and knowledge.

He did seem quite used to receiving foreign visitors. The woman of the house asked us for a small fee of fifteen rupees to cover our room and board and then served us steaming bowls of thukpa. I was used to this simple peasant soup, which in the summer, with vegetables more plentiful, was almost always meatless. I'd been vegetarian since my early teens and travelling in India made it easy. The Hindu pilgrimage places were almost always vegetarian, and if not they'd be sure to let you know. For some reason, I just didn't think to check and devoured three bowls before my brain registered that the big chunks swimming alongside the cubes of high valley onions, in between the blankets of thick barley noodles, and fronds of dark spinach greens were in fact . . . goat.

With the Buddhist injunction against harming life, I just hadn't imagined that butchering would be part of a devout household. In fact, over hundreds of years the valley Buddhists had teamed up with the Dards, whose religion allowed them to serve as the local butchers. Of course, it made sense at this elevation that meat would be part of the diet, and I had seen enough in Buddhist hill stations to have known, but for some reason, I was taken unaware, and it shocked me. To say I was passionate about not eating meat was somewhat of an understatement. I was more than a little inflexible, rabid might be a better word. In my humiliation at crossing my own principles, I felt fury. Like a match waving below the fuse of a bottle rocket, the whizzzz of ego flared up my spine and set my brain on tilt. Deflection might not be one of the fetters in the Pali Canon but it sure was one of mine. That ego voice hissed like a snake ready to strike. I looked over the king's thin face. The fairytale page turned black, "Nothing so royal about all this." That voice snarled in my head. "Just a thin old grandfather in polyester Indian trousers with a filmy pair of eyeglasses. And he eats dead animals, too!"

Dharma is all well and good when we are in our best states of mind. When we are not, that's when the level of our attainment or our immense hubris shows through. I still had so much to tame. At least I had suffered through this side of myself over and over during ten-day silent retreats. I knew I was being unreasonable even if I couldn't stop the machinery of my ego. I bit my tongue, sat on my hands and waited for this flareup to burn itself out. My cheeks burned with embarrassment and shame but no one knew why. I probably just looked pained and uncomfortable, it could have been cramps from our long day's walk. In the king's calm presence, I eventually settled down. He did, in fact, remind me of my grandfather, a thin, gentle, and long-suffering soul. My eyes roamed around the landscape of the room to the vajra and dorje on the altar shelf, silver and copper shapes smithed in the village with care and attention. The message their shapes gave off was balance and moderation. The Buddha taught the middle way, how to live in this world without making waves.

He taught humility and tolerance. I was a little more like a bulldozer or a wrecking ball.

My companion and I were finally excused after several hours and sent upstairs to rest. There were a number of guest rooms, like little monk cells on the top of the house. We each had our own and the rooms, though simple, were much more comfortable than those I'd been staying in. There was a little bedframe with a rope "mattress" on which I laid my pad and sleeping bag. It felt odd to be higher than the ground but nice and much softer. It had been a long day and I still stung from my pride.

The house, sheltered on the eastern face of the mountains, stayed dark in the morning and I rose quite late with a puffy head. I felt the traces of disturbing dreams but couldn't quite remember the details. I met Roger on the rooftop, where he was airing out his tent and repacking his backpack. We talked about the day ahead and disagreed about the distance we should cover. It wasn't consequential, and no reason for friction but I still felt a little ashamed and a little stubborn. He reminded me of my Westernness and at the moment I wasn't liking what I was seeing in myself. That didn't make me an easy companion.

I went back into my room to pack my sleeping bag and change into clean underclothes. It was an excuse to take a little time to reflect on my predicament. Nothing had really happened. I had a principle, I crossed my own lines, I got mad. But I didn't quite know how to get back to the enthusiasm I'd felt before. Being only newly familiar with the dharma can lead to a lot of confused reflection. It's not easy to untangle one's own personality knots. That's why they say we need an enlightened teacher to progress. Mental cul-de-sacs were predictable, even mappable. The Abhidhamma, the detailed Buddhist psychology, lays out the most advanced psychotherapeutic diagnostic treatises on the mind ever developed. But navigating them in real time was a different story. I did try anyway to find an antidote, a right view that would dispel the wrong ones that were causing so much reactivity.

Thinking about my unjust criticism of the king and my irritation with my trekking companion, I scanned the reel of my life: the solitary middle child, the rebel against authority, the thirsty seeker, the independent thinker, the second-wave feminist, the free spirit wanderer, the absorbed poet, the early vegetarian.

Unable to be find one uniform path, filled with anxiety over how I measured up, and hot-collared and rebelling against expectations imposed on me, I grew up feeling perpetually trapped and an outsider no matter where I went or what I did. Caught in the bondage of cyclic existence, I saw that no matter which persona, it was all part of the same maze of self-identity. That's why I had followed the calling to leave everything and journey across India without plans, with only the commitment to be on the path, doing everything I could to reach its ultimate goal.

Amidst all my jumbled identities, each with their own voices and justifications, a half-smothered thought kept rising up, like mist off a hidden spring: "Drop it. There's not enough time in this life. All this just brings unhappiness and fear, sharpen the sword of discrimination and use it with a firm and decisive hand."

Almost like a message emerging, I heard the king's voice reciting his morning torma puja. His dharma bell broke through my confusion, a simple sound calling to the Buddhas. I stepped onto the roof for a moment. Ash-colored snow pigeons paced the dusty yard and the tall mast of white cloth prayer flags shifted in the breeze. A few people gracefully moved about, drying kindling on their roofs or gliding through the alleyways, collecting dung chips in four-sided twig baskets. It was a beautiful morning despite my thoughts.

The woman who was taking care of us invited us to perform the torma puja with the king. The chanting and symbolic gestures were soothing and cosmic. I didn't understand them but I focused on his hands as he formed different mudras, poured water from a small ritual vessel with a long spout over the little tsampa balls. It was a moment of peace before the household came fully to life. When the king finished, we bowed three times and went out, the deep blue eternal knot hanging in the doorway flapping with the endlessness of the awakened one's wisdom and compassion and the interconnectedness of everything in the universe. On the open veranda we found a light breakfast of freshly made chapattis and steaming sweet tea with milk waiting for us.

As space is always freshly appearing
And never filled,
So the mind is without limits
And ever aware.
Gazing with sheer awareness
Into sheer awareness,
Habitual, abstract structures melt
Into the fruitful springtime of Buddhahood.

TILOPA
(988-1069)

Chapter Twelve
A Party & the Highest Mountain Pass

The way back to Pishu seemed shorter than the road over the bridge on the Zanskar River and not as frightening. In Pishu, we returned to the same shy and generous family we had stayed with before, who plied us with special flatbreads, tsampa, and tea. It was to be a day of eating and drinking.

The valley widened and the sun was hot. As we crested a short incline, the section officer we had seen a few days earlier overtook us. He had left his white horse behind him. This time, he was measuring road distances up to Pidmu, stopping everywhere possible to get drunk with his friends, old and new. He led us to a large summer pasture in the middle of nowhere. About twenty people were out in the soft sun, celebrating the summer with chang and song. The yaks grazed out of sight over the mountain, their yogurt, sho, cheese, and milk filling the camp with its inimitable acrid-sweet smell. The section officer introduced us to the others, joking with the young women who tended the older men, stealing a pinch here and there from their buttocks. They laughed, well able to hold their own against any of the men.

He gave orders to one of the men at the fire and soon we were served with heavy barley cakes smeared with sho, which we munched on, punctuated with many glasses of chang. Custom dictated that, each time they were emptied, the glasses must be filled to the brim and then drunk all the way to the bottom. A few hours later, sun still high above us, we set off again, a little unsteady on the trail. My steps weaved side to side, sometimes close to the edge of the cliff. I looked over the side, down the rocky escarpment to the platinum river churning below. The section officer, tipsier than I, barreled his way up to be beside me.

"I want a kiss," he slurred in Zanskari. "I'll give you a stick!" I raised my sturdy walking cane, but I couldn't take his advances too seriously. It all seemed rather humorous. The chang had brightened my spirits and life was good.

Just then, several men from the yak camp caught up with us, the alcohol in their blood giving them extra energy and virility. One dashing man came over and took my bag. Chivalry lived in Zanskar! My usually self-sufficient companion shot me an annoyed look as he struggled under his own heavy load. Feminine advantages over feminist principles, I, with only the slightest twinge of guilt, walked on, burden-free. Without the weight, I felt inches taller. My head floated upwards like a helium balloon and my feet skipped and danced over the rocks. Shoulders free of the constricting harness of my pack, I looked up and around instead of down at my toes and the dusty ground.

The landscape was morphing again. The mountains had taken on a purple hue, painted with midnight violet and light lavender patterns. A little town of flour mills sprouted up just before Pidmu, several dozen grinding huts squatting like toadstools on the tributaries to the main river. Our friend led us to a big house full of a dozen men drinking chang as darkness fell. It was an exquisite twilight, but we sat inside a smoky room, Urdu news playing on the second radio I had listened to in a month, the first being at Moti and Krishna's. With the greenish light of kerosene lanterns, I was able to write as I drank, almost like home and those familiar long nights of bleary-eyed writing chasing wisps of insights and the stories unfolding in my mind.

Being inside and around a radio felt more like life in

the West. In the valley, I was living closer to the elements. Could I replicate that once I reached the larger towns again? I doubted it. Progress has a way of eroding simpler ways of living. Almost without choice, once those accouterments come into being, they become a given. I didn't miss electricity, water in pipes, a refrigerator, a grocery store. Though I did miss a toilet much of the time! Could I live without electricity in America? Theoretically yes, but I couldn't imagine it. It wouldn't feel the same. I tried to picture what I would go back to. My heart ached for something I couldn't describe. I felt nostalgic for what I was in the midst of. The future I reached into felt precarious, ephemeral, tinged with sadness compared to sitting safe with strangers by the fire, eating, talking, singing, laughing.

By our third gallon of chang, I stopped writing and surveyed the room. We sat in the large central chamber of the house, off of which opened four good-size rooms. Religious texts bound in orange, red, and yellow cloth jutted out from shelves that lined the walls of one of the rooms. There were a lot of texts, maybe a Rinpoche was part of the extended family. The faces in the room were long and a little angular, their ancestry from a slightly different background. Eyes bright, their teeth gleamed white through the smoke and dust in the air. I loved the way the men wore their hair, their thick black braids tied on top of their heads, their turquoise and silver earrings. They cut handsome figures. At some point, we tired, and unrolled our bedrolls, I in one of the rooms off the kitchen area, most of the men in the main room, and all fell asleep.

The next morning, Roger and I started early, it was going to be a big day and I could feel in our efficiency and decisive pace, we were ready for the challenge. Destination— up. Up and over a high pass. This was the part of trekking I relished, the rhythm, the push, the strength it took and the strength it made. The canyon narrowed, rough ridges bled into the mountain tops, strong rugged lines defined our way, refreshing after the wide, dusty stretch we'd been walking. I could feel the chill off the river water as we crossed a small bridge. So elemental. Hot sun. Cold water. Hard rocks. Step by step. Walking, a meditation in motion, clearing out the complexity and the karma of lifetimes, wiping the dust away, polishing the mirror of consciousness clean. Hard sometimes, easy sometimes, revelatory always if I looked deeply enough. This was my work, to make it all count for the long haul, even if I didn't really know what I was supposed to do next.

We began the long ascent up the side face of one of the mountains, not the one that held the pass in its saddle, but a lower fold in the range that would carry us closer to Parfi La. We would have to go up, and then down, up and then down again, and perhaps one more ridge before the pass. Each ridge gained a little more elevation. But the up and down made the way long. The slope was slippery scree; my ankles twisted and pebbles rolled into my shoes. A little envy rose up in my throat, with its sour aftertaste; Roger had quite the advantage with his high-tech Swiss mountain boots. Contentment can be wiped out with one stray grasping, with envy that's not quelled. The more I watched my mind, the more impurities I saw. It seemed a ridiculously long journey to enlightenment with all the debris in my mind.

About an hour outside of Hanumil, a tiny town of just a few houses, we found a perfect beach by the riverbank and stopped for a quick tea and European treats. I felt shy not having anything to give him in return, especially having coveted what he had, as if I still thought I was more deserving. The stories about the Buddha are all well and good, that is until you measure up your own life against them and find yourself falling so far short.

According to the Jataka Tales, the Buddha's last incarnation before becoming the fully awakened one was as a wandering ascetic in the hills. Walking along a cliff's edge, he heard the mewing of baby tiger cubs. Looking down the drop he saw a mama tigress, emaciated, with a litter sucking at her dry teats. The tigress was spent from birthing, her paws lay limp by her body, so crazed with exhaustion and hunger, needing strength to feed her young, she was eyeing her own offspring as food, not realizing what she was doing. The Buddha contemplated the suffering of the body, the depths to which it can trick us, and the consideration of his own healthy body and what its purpose was. Considering long term good, how to inspire others to generosity, and how to circumvent the wrongdoing of the hungry tigress, the Buddha is said to have seen the solution. Exploding with great joy, he hurled himself over the cliff so his body could feed the tigress and she could generate milk for her young. That act of compassion was said in some sources to be his perfection of bodhicitta, exchanging self for other. This was the final paramita he needed to attain. In his next life, as the fully Awakened One, he would revolutionize the path of human evolution and create an order of awakened nuns and monks whose impact and example of discrimination, understanding, and compassion continues some 2500 years later.

 With the contemplation of those standards in mind, I continued to walk, feeling somewhat small and not very far along the path to awakening. The physical route carried us upward more than forward. Roger went ahead, his elastic legs stretching forward, his pack hiding most of his body. I followed some hundred yards behind, trailing behind on the series of narrow switchbacks that traversed the side of the mountain. Out of nowhere, a storm thundered. In the way these mountains had, the idyllic Shangri-La day turned menacing. Shivering on the edge of a cliff, hard rain pelted us, challenging our ascent. Even though Parfi La was one of the lower passes, just shy of 4,000 meters, it stood guard of the monastery on the other side, challenging those who wanted to enter.

 Roger and I found a rock overhang and we took shelter underneath it for a time. The storm passed as quickly as it had appeared, barely getting the dry ground wet, and the afternoon softened. From this point on, the terrain became more intense and even more beautiful. The mountain wrinkles dug deeper, and the trail practically kissed the outer edge of the cliff. I ran my fingers along the roughness of the inner side of the rock. I was learning through all my senses to read the folds and furrows of the earth, divining what we would face in the next few days by looking down the valley and along the spiked peaks all around us. I had come a long way since that first day meandering unsteadily on the goat paths at the entrance of the valley. Then I spent the bulk of my steps backtracking, unsure, more or less lost most of the time. The mountains were becoming more a part of me or I was becoming more a part of them, embedded and embraced, not a marble rolling randomly around their surface.

A thin beige line worn into the rocks painted our trail to the height of the pass. Wild pink rose bushes jutted out from narrow outcroppings, their petals set off by the shimmering abalone river more than a thousand feet below. We were way above the tree line but here in Zanskar, flowers seemed to magically appear out of nowhere. Ascending soothed me, a methodical progression. Climbing up is often a wordless endeavor, hour after hour of straining thigh muscles, and twinging calves. Thumbs stuck in my pack straps, I pulled on them as if I could will myself forward. These moments are solitary. We all have to push through our own inertia, the weight that anchors us to our lower natures. I felt my determination and my intention rising in me like a growl.

The burst of conviction lasted a short while, and the ascent lasted longer. A bucket rattling at the bottom of an empty well, I scraped for reserves. It had been ten hours since we set out a long sunrise ago. The last stretch of several hundred meters jumped almost vertically through fingers of rocks. We hoisted ourselves up, finding cracks for finger and toe holds. I could feel the pounding of my heart in my inner ears. The focus brought freshness, excitement, immediacy. One last push and I hoisted myself up. A strong wind gushed around me. My feet planted themselves at the scraggly narrow top of the pass. Ascent!

A panorama of snowcaps spread all around us. Frayed prayer flags attached to the corners of the chorten flapped in the wind. The top of a pass was all swirling elements, dizzying drops. Over worked muscles twinged and shivered. The sunset decorated the sky, unfurling festival banners of clouds. Auspicious signs shimmered all around us. The mountains embraced us. I felt the rush of victory and accomplishment. Roger and I whooped and shouted, widely grinning at each other. There was barely space for two and it felt like a giant eagle could pluck us off the top. No more than ten or fifteen minutes to celebrate, we straddled the ridge and started the steep descent down the other side. I kept shouting into the wind, smiling so that the gusts dried my mouth and my lips stuck, frozen to my teeth.

We skipped and stumbled our way down. My knees protested the hard contact each step, but my heart laughed, running and leaping with abandon. A couple hour jog down made quick work of our full day's ascent. A deserted yak corral in a ravine sculpted into the rock by snow runoff awaited us. We cooked a long and large dinner and talked until the moon set. It was so good to sleep under the stars. Constellations twirled and danced. There is magic in this world, we open the doors to it with our own effort and sacrifice.

*The polymorphous Mara
may approach the vulnerable practitioner in various
guises—during meditative trance, dream, or even
waking state.
The spiritually polluting influence of Mara
can also manifest as a heavenly sounding voice. ...
Mara can magically or hypnotically project various
earthly
or heavenly forms or can act through unsuspecting
human beings.*

PRAJNAPARAMITA SUTRAS
(100 BCE – 500 CE)

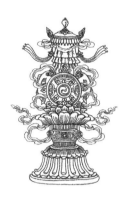

Chapter Thirteen
Mountain Bandits & A Glacial Shadow

There's a certain stage in a journey when things start to blend one into another. Morning into midday into afternoon into night. That halfway-ish point, where the start of the journey feels long ago and the end is not yet in sight. It's mesmerizing and mysterious. Anything can happen, and sometimes it does. We were walking the next day and the path was opening and welcoming.

There were all kinds of intriguing smaller paths, that led to even more remote villages and monasteries. At one junction of slope and river, I saw an enticing canyon leading off to the west, curling around a corner and out of sight. That was a way even less traveled, but I was committed to reaching Lingshet and so turned away from the beckoning unknown. A narrow wooden bridge spanned the water, the searing midday sun shone in silver and copper flecks in the wrinkles of the water. We stopped on a rocky beach at the far shore to bathe. Separating, Roger and I went to our own private bathing spots to enjoy the grooming I took for granted my whole life with daily hot showers and thick, clean towels. I unbound my hair from the confines of two plaits and dipped my cup into the ice water. I doused my head and scrubbed out the dust and dried sweat. The water sent shocks through my body and pounding into my ears. The head is always the hardest part to clean. Once my hair smelled fresh, I twisted it into a bun and stripped to wash my body. The wind felt good on my skin but I found myself quite shy. In the West, I bathed naked in the woods, but I had grown accustomed to hiding my body in Asia, modestly becoming clean, like the Indian women, with two and a half meters of cloth wrapped around me. Muscles half-tense, I dried in the wind, straining to hear hooves or footsteps. Finally, I gave into my inhibitions and dressed quickly, shaking my head at myself for my worries here in the middle of isolated mountain folds. To be clean was pure joy, even when I crawled back into the dusty skin of the same clothes.

The sky was a perfectly clear deep blue, like a movie set. The air was so dry it burned my nostrils and scorched my throat as it went down. I breathed hard. The next stretch of path was the steepest I had ever climbed. I looked down, straight down; my camera couldn't record the steepness. Everything looked flat. But it wasn't. Hour after hour I watched the river shrink into a lead-colored hair below, then it was left behind as I wound east around the side of the cliff. The slope dizzied me. I wanted to hug the side, but I forced myself forward, inching along. Roger shouted encouragement but I blanched pale. The trail was barely as wide as my foot's width, on top of sand and scree, and with a thousand-meter drop. Vertigo is a devious fear, it grabs you by the scruff of the neck from behind, and shakes you till all your joints knock against each other.

Turning into the elbow between two peaks, I was not sorry to leave the precarious edge. Though I could force myself to walk through my vertigo, I much preferred to have both feet planted on a wide patch of earth. The entire area we were entering was a hodgepodge of ridges and mountains, flung topsy turvy like a pile of laundry fresh from the dryer waiting to be sorted, smoothed, and folded. Grey, blue, silver, beige, auburn, rust, copper, and mocha, some fluffy, others smooth, sharp, powdery, rough, or scratchy. Each pinnacle shimmered in the heat and thin air. The geometric patterns in the cliffs moved as I studied them. The earth still groaned from the labor that birthed these young mountains into being.

It was a safer but rough next section, scrambling across smaller rockslides interspersed with trail. The hours ticked by and afternoon shadows great longer. The rocks were black and orange like chunks of rusted iron. Dogging downwards the trail met a stream, melted snow runoff from the massifs. Light green grasses grew around the water and some herders had set up summer pastures on the high-altitude marsh. They called this place Upper Netshe or Snertse for short. It was a very strange place.

I had come to expect a Zanskari warm welcome. This time I was in for a surprise. The herders had vicious dogs that frightened the wits out of me. The mongrels wore thick black manes matted with burrs and twigs. Their protectiveness began as low rumblings deep in their gut and built up momentum, like a landslide, until huge boulders of their growl erupted past their sharp yellow incisors. We crept up at twilight, a time when the dogs were most suspicious, skittering about anticipating the moonrise. Several blackened and scruffy teenagers came down from a hill above us, smacking the yaks into the stone corrals with stout sticks and loud yells. They offered to sell us a ladle of curd for three rupees but seemed to be more inclined towards looting than trading. They may have been animal tenders, but they felt more like wild mountain pirates. The sight of them raised gooseflesh on my arms and I was grateful not to be alone. The overseer of the camp was an older, wily man. His eyes bulged out of his head like a Pekingese dog as he ogled and grunted, sniffing and walking in a circle around us. He cursed the hounds and pelted a handful of rocks in their direction. I heard a few thuds as they found their marks, followed by the whimper of the beasts. I asked the man where we could sleep. He slunk his head into his shoulders and cackled. Raising his arm with one bony finger peeking out of his black cloak sleeve, he pointed to a flat circle past the yak shelters. Then he shouted at the boys and they laughed, a dark and leering laugh. He barked an order, and they scampered down to their stone hut chanting the verses of what could only be a high-mountain bandit song.

Roger and I climbed above the camp and found a Western-style tent occupied by a lanky sullen French girl and a Nepali boy. We moved past them with barely a greeting. It was cold. The wind cut through my clothes and bit my cheeks. We decided to both share the tent. Roger was tired and irritable and left me to make dinner. I could all but see a cackling irascible spirit just beyond my firepit, puffing uneven gusts of life-sucking breath, blowing away what little warmth the flames gave off. In the end, the food remained half-cooked and not very tasty. We ate in grim silence as the wind whistled eerily down the cleavage of the peaks, sweeping through our camp spot and sending the dogs into fits of howling. Stars pricked the sky like hard needles, their twinkling witchlike. I had been annoyed with Roger during dinner, his sullenness increasing my chagrin at the tasteless meal I'd prepared. Some shadow had fallen on us and whatever it was, it seemed to blanket that entire area.

If I had learned one thing from that first ten-day retreat in the Kathmandu Valley with the Tibetan Geshe, it was to practice gratitude as a method of purification. Thanks would not only provide protection but it would uncover blessings obscured by malevolent spirits. I looked at Roger sitting at the door of the tent, back curled against the outside and gave thanks for the day, for the protection of being with another, for a sustaining meal, and for the opportunity to practice. I prayed for the darkness to pass and for us to move quickly through it, and for the strength to make the high passes we would reach tomorrow. I also prayed for sleep to come quickly, I didn't want to keep watch over whatever spirits were spinning their web tonight. Tibetan Buddhism has a host of wrathful deities, technically images that represent states of mind and spiritual strengths, but on another level they also serve as deities that act. These fierce and angry looking buddhas represent manifestations of their peaceful counterparts and protect against malevolent forces. The rings of fire around their bodies incinerate ignorance and evil. Under their feet are the crushed bodies of anger, greed, delusion, and harm of all kinds. In the bucolic enclave of Dharamsala, I didn't really understand the need. At this moment, with the pale green light of an ominous almost full moon reflecting off the glacial ice, I most certainly did.

Sleep did not come quickly or easily. It was an awful night. I tossed and turned, finally dozing off only to wake in the dark hours, thirst searing through me and no water. My skin cried out for liquid, my forehead was burning, and my lips were puffed and cracking. The dogs yapped and howled. I couldn't step out of the tent from fear. I wished Roger would wake but was paralyzed and couldn't reach over to shake him. I lay back in anguish. Three hours later, Roger woke me. He too had woken with tormenting thirst and had climbed down to the stream. The moon had slid behind the mountain cap, it was darker than dark with just a tiny bit of light from the stars mirrored in the snow. The dogs were finally silent. I took the water bottle, my eyes misty with gratitude. Something was not quite right in this camp. My ignorance of the history of that glacial mouth and the demons and spells cast there probably helped me stay put through that night. At 4,000 meters, predawn winds cut straight to the bone, even in our tent. I lay back down into the soft fluff of my bag, tucked my knees into my chest, wrapped my arms around myself, and rocked myself into a light sleep. Close to five, when the first stars began to fade from the firmament, we packed up and began to walk.

The suchness of pure presence
does not emigrate, migrate, transmigrate, or emanate.
There is no division within pure presence.
There is no multiplication of pure presence.
Suchness cannot be enumerated,
even with the numeral one.

PRAJNAPARAMITA SUTRAS
(100 BCE – 500 CE)

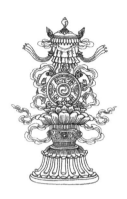

Chapter Fourteen
Revelation on the Top of the World

The spiritual journey is often like walking through a tunnel cut into the deepest earth. That pull from the heart leads forward, into the darkness, with really only one direction possible: the one you take. Veils and mirages, reflections of lower states of mind pop out and evaporate, sometimes leaving inspiration, sometimes leaving shivers in the soul. In the middle of the tunnel, it looks mostly dark on both sides. So I kept walking.

As the day burned off the shadows of the previous night, I forgot about the scene that faded into a surreal haze. Excitement started to bubble up, effervescent energy pinging in my veins. I was nearing the highest pass of my journey. While I'd been going up and down, up and down, uuuuuuup and down, 16,000 feet or 4,900 meters is impressive for any trekker. Higher than the highest peak in the Rocky Mountains, I was going up and over with my scrappy sneakers, carrying my own pack, with no ropes or gear other than my balance and my hardening thigh muscles. I had no doubt I would make it. It was just how long it would take, how hard it would be, and how much I'd have to wrestle with my mind. In the middle of the Zanskari Valley, it's not like there is much choice. To get out of the valley, I'd have to scale the pass. I was excited. I was proud. I wanted to reach that peak. Aspiration and desire can run very close to one another.

The climb started gradually. It didn't feel like much more than any other day. My anticipation drove me. Entering into a narrow valley most of the morning, my steps crunched the snow in the mountain bank's shadow. Happiness sparkled in my mind like sunlight on a rippled lake top. Roger was behind me and today, as far as I could see, was empty and wide open. The arms of the mountains reached out to embrace me, step by step I snuggled into her furrows, till she swallowed me up. My heart embraced her back, hard. A pair of eagles whirled in the sky above, dancing protection and blessing.

It was a long and beautiful way up to Hanumil La. I stopped and pulled out my Indian army map, soft as felt from use, and rubbed my fingers over the contours leading up to this gateway to the beyond. The trail resembled pretty much every other meter I had walked and yet this section was different, more. I walked the hypotenuse of the mountainside, feeling the geometry of millions of years of the earth's birthing. Geologists say that the Himalayas were formed by the crash of two great tectonic plates, but I felt like these majestic stone beings were more like the children come from the womb of the earth, brought into being not by collision but by fierce contractions and the powerful push of love.

As I rose, my mind got clearer and clearer. The sky in midday loses its color and washes out into brilliant transparency. My thoughts felt the same, burned into thinness, so I could all but dissolve into the emptiness behind everything. Out on the edges of the earth and the mind there are no fixed reference points. You can arbitrarily choose which markers to measure your way but they are only projections of the mind. That's where training comes in. Training and practice provide the chortens that reveal the reliable gateways to higher consciousness. Without that, our center of gravity, our mental habits sink to the mundane or worse, and fill the void.

By my eye, I still had about eight hours ahead. At first it seemed so close, such a short distance given the great body of earth I was stroking with my steps. Just eight hours to climb what has taken some seventy million years to form. I wanted to savor every second, drink it in. Just as I thought that, my inner clock changed the way it told time. Hours started to stretch like taffy. Quarter hours inched forward at a glacial pace. At first, I did mantras to keep going. Then, my mind bored, I switched to those childhood chants that made long school trip bus rides pass. "Ninety-nine bottles of beer on the wall" counted time and marched my feet forward. I sing-songed down to one, several times. Then there was nothing to keep me going. My mind got milky, liquidy. Time slowed to treacle in the winter, barely moving. The pass was still hours away, the chortens at the top no longer visible from this angle just below.

This was the solitary section. Like meditating through the night, I was in that space that was darkest before dawn, the three AM time, when the mind plays tricks and Mara sends out his demons and temptresses to move the mind away from enlightenment. I watched the thinning sky above, a few gossamer cloud wisps appeared. Maybe the devas would pull me up by their long sashes. The middle of the day has that same quality as darkness of deep night. Long, shifting, illusory. Shadows narrowed, flattening the landscape, playing tricks with distance and perspective. My thoughts were as uninspired as the remnants of a bowl of oatmeal left on the counter, cold, picked over. I would have thought the closer I got, the loftier my contemplations would be. In reality, it was so much the opposite. Three-quarters of the way up, and I was running out of things to think. It wasn't inspired emptiness. Just used-up emptiness. How did the monks do it on their multi-year, multi-decade retreats? I was like the youngest child in the four questions of Passover, I didn't yet know what to ask. I had so much study to do to know how to fill my mind with just the questions to contemplate, let alone the answers. The idea of long retreats, really long, at least the three-year, three-month, three-day foundational Nyingma retreats felt within reach in my image of myself. But the mind is a tricky thing to put under the rarefied discipline of practice. Practice is a structure that opens up rather than tightens down. The mind does better with boundaries, with a container. This freedom beckoning was so very open. Unformed. The idea is exultant. The path austere.

I wasn't nearly as far along as I thought was, practically and spiritually. The sense of just beginning added drag to my step. Our minds can make us believe just about anything is the truth, when all the time we're still working with a partial deck. How can we possibly know all that goes into the karmic momentum that brought us into the lives we're in right now? Maybe we're like the Buddha in one of his final births, almost there. Maybe we just climbed out of the primordial sludge of a lower realm, where we'd been wandering, suffering for countless eons until a tiny bit of grace, a little bit of merit ripens and catapults us into a human birth where we have the chance, if we work hard, stay focused, and practice, to penetrate illusion and burst into the clear seeing, realizing the infinite heart, and abiding in indescribable joy.

Regardless of what our minds are telling us, life is happening, right now. We're always in prime time, whether we appreciate it or not. As Ram Dass famously said, we're always here, it's always now. A little part of me was appreciating that even as my thoughts oscillated from confidence and ecstasy to self-doubt and discouragement. I kept going, step by step, through the doldrums, through the inspired visions. Lost in thought, I didn't even notice that I had climbed up for hours and hours, till just one little stretch separated me from the knife edge of the ridge, and the pass that would reveal infinity.

The smell of the air changed. At different elevations the texture of the air feels different, the scent it leaves in the back of the throat changes. I could taste the height before I noticed it visually. Looking around me, my heart caught. According to my Indian army map, I was steps below the peak, 16,000 feet above sea level. The incline of the last couple hundred meters softened and hugged the ridge like a ramp up to heaven.

One dusty foot in front of another. All of the sudden, from eight hours and the bottom of the valley, the chorten marking the only way over this section of the mountain range was under my hand. Cool stones reaching to meet my palms as my hands connected with its surface. Wild goat horns on either end of the four-foot chorten curled in welcome like a floral bouquet and two frayed white prayer flags snapped their blessings in the wind. I'd made the ascent!

Standing, I was the highest thing around me. Three long lines of razor tooth peaks stretched out in front of me. The cuts of the valleys, the memory of the rough rivers below were all I could see of the floor. Standing on solid rock, looking down at the tops of snow peaks is an orientation hard to describe. Language, too abstract for the closeness, does little to transmit the immediacy. I was one more element, part of this living world, inseparable from the vast cosmos out of which emerged these massive and intimate formations, carved over millions and millions of years by each of the elements—wind, fire, rock, and water—in an ongoing flow of unending change.

My chest ached. My heart pounded, whether from the awe or the altitude, it was hard to tell. My insides were restructuring, stretching open to the vastness all around. Taking in the dizzying expanse, I held my arms out like an eagle, my mind's eye tracing the long legs of the mountains spread out beneath me. Before me, the Tethys Himalaya sprawled in all her glory, resting on the chaise lounge of the top of the world. Her feminine curves, her masculine ferocity, her aged snow hair, her child rock ornaments, every aspect of her perfect, sublime.

My mind stopped. The fullness and treasure of it exploded in all my cells. When the Tibetans describe the nectar of the gods feeding you with happiness, this is what they must mean. All was good. All had always been good. All will always be good. Earthquakes, avalanches, and conflagrations notwithstanding, goodness remains the substratum underlying all. At the top of the world, goodness vibrates in all its brilliance and clarity. Like powdery snow blowing off the ridge and disappearing into the sky, every last nagging question and self-doubt I ever had evaporated. So vanished, they never were. It had all been a mirage, a play of consciousness that formed temporarily only to un-form again. Everything is always complete and full as it is and always in a phase of forming and un-forming. Life, change, and impermanence coexist, inseparable from this reality of already-fullness, already-completeness, wholeness. It is not just a backdrop, it is the essence of all that is and always has been. As the Buddha declared atop Vultures' Peak, form is emptiness and emptiness is form. Form is none other than emptiness and emptiness is none other than form. The forming and changing is none other than the oneness, inclusive of all that is, was, and will be. It all started crashing in, like the matrix, seen through.

It struck me. What it all meant. My mind downshifted. Snapped.

Breathing the rarefied air at the top of the pass and looking out over the spine of the snow mountains, everything flashed together in a crescendo of resolution. The whole illusion of grasping for anything, reaching for anything else to make me full was not only unnecessary, it was the expression of what created the suffering, the alienation, the longing for Home. Even the aching to cross another pass, climb another mountain, or see another breathtaking moonrise became clear for what it was: a subtle form of grasping, postponing, delaying the acceptance of the eternal present. There was nowhere to go and nothing to do. There never could be. How can you move towards what you already are? Could you take the wetness out of water, the coldness out of snow? the hardness out of rock? Infinite consciousness is our nature. Any movement to attain, any movement towards what was next was a movement away from the perfection that already is.

I laughed, filled with happiness and shock. When the Zanskaris say we all already have Buddha nature, they aren't kidding. They mean it literally.

The challenge of my journey and the worry of trying to figure out what to do next was all part of the play, the *lila*, the temporary formation of waves on the surface of being. These fireworks in my heart exploded the little vessels of plans and desires; unfinished business; unresolved angst of my adolescence, everything, including the ambition to climb one more pass higher than the last, see one more valley, or drink from one more crystal glacial stream.

The timeless revelation probably lasted less than ten minutes in linear time, but it was so much more than that. It left an irreparable crack to a different vantage point on existence. As much as that opening might seem to knit back together, a hairline fissure would remain until I was ready to never go back to the world of separation and duality. Buddhists say we prepare lifetimes for this, for that moment when we are ready to step off the karmic wheel of endless suffering and becoming, grasping for completion, living from birth to death to birth never realizing that what we seek already is. It takes a mature soul to give up everything and realize everything without going anywhere or changing anything or doing anything different. Awakening is an entirely different world, in exactly the world as it has always been.

Heaven and hell, as Emanuel Swedenborg wrote, exist side-by-side; it all has to do with our minds and the thoughts we choose to follow. The demons at the gates of the glacier in Netse, the panorama of the snow peaks stretching out in front of me into the horizon, the turquoise-blue sky, and the wild rich air all mixed together. My whirling thoughts came to a standstill. In the clouds above me I could all but see Manjushri, hand raised, waving his sword of wisdom, cutting through delusion. In the other hand, he lifted the lotus of transformation. All around him bodhisattvas strummed their lutes, issuing sacred sound, filling the void with blessings of protection. They danced the mudras of equipoise and victory over ignorance. The whoosh of their robes was closer than close.

Then, they were gone.

I had seen a different realm, however briefly. As I have come to understand, even the smallest glimpse of infinity is still infinite. It is enough to reshape the rest of a noble human birth.

The completely open nature
Of all dimensions and events
Is a rainbow always occurring
Yet never grasped.

The way of Mahamudra
Creates no closure.
No strenuous mental effort
Can encounter this wide open way.
The effortless freedom of awareness
Moves naturally along with it.

TILOPA
(988-1069)

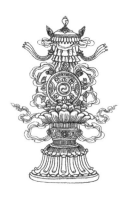

Chapter Fifteen
Cliff Dwellers & Dancers

As is the way in the mountains and of life, ascent is just part of a flow. Soon enough, I was once again heading down the very steep northern side. My mind feeling stretched, I remained in an altered state. When Roger had arrived at the top of the pass, we celebrated briefly, though for me marking any moment in the eternal present that stretched in all directions without end didn't really make sense. He and I were in the same location but in two different worlds. I didn't try to explain. I didn't really have the words. The immediacy and intimacy crushing in on what I had thought was me made it hard to carry on conversation or even describe what I was experiencing. How does water, immersed in water, describe itself? There is only one.

Roger went ahead. Striding quickly, soon he was out of sight. The afternoon sun burned. There were switchbacks and ridges and I traveled downward for a time only to head up again, across Chapskang La, another pass, then down, and finally across high verdant fields, reaching Lingshet at 7:30. I was so tired I could barely walk. I was happy to see villagers, it had been a long stretch sleeping out in the open or in wayfarer's huts. I found Roger and a house where they served us tsampa, taro, chapattis, subji, thukpa, and chang and gave us a place inside to sleep.

Though my body and mind were beyond spent, I couldn't sleep. My torso and limbs hummed. The inner peaks I had climbed were filling my system full of energy that seemed not only physical and, in some way, not just me. In many spiritual systems, there are maps of subtle currents, not quite physical, not quite mental that chart degrees of insight or capacity. While I couldn't say what I was experiencing, all I knew was that another type of energy was rising up and flowing through channels I hadn't known about before. Everything that I'd heard about the *lungs* or winds that flow up and down subtle chutes or channels when I sat in the ten-day Guhyasamaha teaching with the Dalai Lama in Dharamsala made sense. When I was listening to his intricate description of colors and energy flowing up one side of the heart and down another, merging, forming, dispersing, and reforming I understood it to be a metaphor to train the mind. I imagined the visualizations to be a discipline that conveyed subtle philosophical principles and relationships to higher states of consciousness through imagery. I suppose it is that too but I had flattened out the teachings I was hearing into dimensions I was familiar with. The practice was also literal and the energy coursing through my body now wasn't imagined.

It also wasn't real in the way I was used to. It wasn't physical in the sense I feel my heart pumping when I exert myself, or the way my blood pounds in my ears when I am excited or scared. This was different. It was specific, precise, and oddly nonlocal. It burned in an intangible sort of way. Not unpleasant, nor pleasant exactly either, it almost hurt the way ecstasy can be too much, too intense. I felt like millions of burst awake particles of consciousness were carrying on a conversation with each other that I could overhear in a sensory way, but not understand. I was glad to be inside the Zanskari home and not entirely alone.

I woke in the morning, happy and a little disoriented. Rushing to the next point on the map felt arbitrary, I was not even really sure where I would be trying to get to or why. I was not confused, everything seemed just a little . . . different. I stood up, stretching my legs. Contentment was so thick in the room I could hardly move and so much energy was still coursing through me I could hardly stay inside my bones. It made sense to stay put for a few days. I liked it in this town. It was the most beautiful village I'd been to.

I let Roger know my plans over breakfast by the family hearth. He was ready to keep walking. It had been a good chapter and now we each had our own journeys to follow. As is with travelers, you fall in step together for a time, then the strands of your karma part and each goes forward according to their own unfolding. Part of the code of the road was to accept the fate that crosses your path with another. You continue your journey together for a while, accommodating each other, strangers who might never have connected in a regular life situation but whom fate threw together. Maybe you met to resolve karma from the past, maybe to connect again in this birth. You could never be sure when one of these chance encounters will turn out to be a life-changing event or cause you to turn down a path you never would have discovered and end up somewhere, decades later, in a completely different life. Or it could be a chance encounter that lasts a little while, then burns itself out like a stick of incense, leaving a little tail of ash and a warm smell in the air. So it was with our encounter. We had walked in step with one another for a time, harmonious, if not exactly close in the ordinary sense of the word, and now it was time for something new to unfold. We said goodbye, wishing each other well. The brilliant sky shone, empty of trace.

I explored the village, feeling the expansiveness, the air crackling with clarity, every form and the shape between the forms feeling fuller than full with emptiness. The village was surrounded by verdant fields of young barley that swayed and glistened in the light wind. I could see the passes I'd crossed in the distance to the south, the ring of high peaks encircling the valley like a royal crown. Over to the north on the side of the cliff perched a magnificent set of white stucco structures. They seemed so small, like an insect's egg sack clinging to a tree. It was the renowned Lingshet Gompa.

Lingshet Gompa is a stately monastery founded by a disciple of Je Tsongkhapa, the great master, revered by all Tibetan Buddhists and especially by the Gelugpa lineage, the line of the Dalai Lama. The set of prayer halls, kitchens, and residences I was looking at were built in the 1440s on a site of earlier cave monasteries. The founder, Sherab Zangpo had crossed the same Hanumil La pass on one of his journeys through the valley. He was a great builder, credited with establishing both Phuktal Monastery and Karsha Gompa, the large monastery I'd vacillated back and forth between visiting and not in what seemed like a lifetime ago. Sherab Zangpo is said to have crossed Hanumil La and seen a great light blazing on the side of the mountain. That spot now forms the center of the main shrine room at the gompa, and the energy is said to be continually charged by that most auspicious light. In 1779, the king of Ladakh gave the land surrounding the monastery to the third incarnation of Ngari Rinpoche. The current Ngari Rinpoche is the Dalai Lama's youngest brother. Having come to Zanskar after living in Dharamsala, the seat of the Dalai Lama, the Gelugpa associations felt familiar, like home. Happiness filled me.

I walked the half hour across fields then skirted the mountainside over to the gompa where I was so stuffed with *ka-lak,* a fermented tsampa mixed with sho, and tea I could hardly move. They ladled it out to everyone. There was a big puja going on. What luck! Or maybe they have celebrations almost all of the time? This is one of the largest monasteries in the valley, with some sixty monks and some recluses doing many year retreats in the caves nearby. One day, I thought, I would love to give up everything and settle into the world of inner discipline and discovery for a long time. For the years they say it takes to deepen in meditation. Though nothing is familiar, it feels like I know this place, like I'd been here before. I wondered if you could have karmic memories. Remembrances that aren't quite literal from one life to the next, more like rememberings of things that are spiritually familiar, resonant of your path now, like a meandering of the heart that stumbles on itself and feels like it has known itself for a very long time.

Lingshet Gompa is one of the spiritual centers of the valley. The atmosphere felt super charged and the non-stop chanting added a rumbling undercurrent and energetic crescendo. Old and young came from the town, dressed in their finest, wearing all their jewels, and the monks filled the guests' cloth sacks with tsampa and poured endless tea. All day long, people filled the hallways and sat on the rooftops of the temple. Malas moved in their dry brown hands, prayer wheels circled with their own momentum, channeling the momentum of the earth's centripetal force, hurling out mantras on the currents of air to bless everything far and wide.

The mantras are the monk's eagles, with wings that shadow everything under them as they swoop down valleys, snake along rivers and rise above houses. Blessings. More blessings. Blessings for peace. Blessings for awakening. Blessings of gratitude to all the buddhas, bodhisattvas, and revered teachers. The chanting echoed with force from within the main temple room. The drums sounded loud and low. Thump. Thump. Thump. Thump. I sat, cross-legged near the entrance of the main temple room for a long time. When I tired of the puja, I went to one of the rooms down the hall where two older monks were sewing yellow and red Benares silk cloaks for the Buddha statues. They were attentive to their work and peaceful. They didn't pay too much attention to me; we were all just quiet, without artifice. The meditative current was strong, I felt it from the inside as much as from the outside. The only interruptions were the young monks with their huge chai pots and bags of tsampa, they would come around and fill our cups liberally, quietly and respectfully, again and again.

There were many segments of the puja, followed by a big procession of instruments through the main temple room. Six monks, with their *dung chen*, long horns three meters or so in length, blasted their coded messages to the deities from the roof of the gompa. Around 1,000 years ago, similar horns were said to have been sounded from somewhere deep in Tibet to invite the great scholar and realizer Atisha to bring the Buddha's teachings to the land of the snow. The tones, multi-layered and commanding, traveled and echoed down the valley, reverberating off the sides of the mountains. Maybe beings in other dimensions could hear them too. Maybe even those suffering in lower realms. Maybe amidst the cacophony of the hell realms a little sound could penetrate and carry with it the reminder of the possibility of wisdom, compassion, and awakened consciousness—those karmic imprints that could lead to release from eons of suffering, that could lead to a better rebirth in a realm where it's possible to hear the dharma, practice the dharma, and attain enlightenment.

Whatever this puja was about, whatever its prayers invoked, and however unusual or common its practice, to me, it was magic. For the entire day I felt encased in a cloud of a meditative process that I didn't understand and couldn't explain. I didn't even want to try to explain to myself, the prayers and mystique pulled me in, and I kept letting go. It felt like I was meant to be here and was meant to sit in the midst of this loud and relentless stream of chanting. I was exactly where I should be. At exactly the right time. As if nothing else could possibly have occurred at this particular moment, this year, this month, this summer day.

Sometimes we experience those moments that seem like everything is so perfectly in place, choices that seem like a trick of the mind. Was it really choice? Destiny couldn't have had it any other way. I let the puja carry me, sitting, sometimes meditating, sometimes watching, sometimes riding the raft of prayer in the rapids of this indescribable energy. When you're in the rapids, water surging all around, there's only one way to go. Stay in the center of the current and ride it out. The energy welled up behind my eyes, and I continued to have a sense of an inner world I couldn't access with my ordinary mind opening up. A parallel world, a world behind the mirror. It didn't matter that I didn't understand. Maybe I would later, maybe it would simply leave imprints and influence me in ways that would ripen in their own time. In Buddhism they say there are many layers to the teachings, visible and secret or hidden ones. You understand the different layers when you are ready to. You may realize the nature of consciousness, time, and causation if you've created the karmic readiness to see. If not now, seeds of wisdom are still lodged to open in future births. Either way, keep practicing, keep accumulating good merit.

Townspeople walked in and out, some sitting in the hallways, malas clicking, lips moving in prayer. Little children stood nearby, eyes big, awed. Bigger children ran around collecting whatever boys collect and chasing each other through corkscrew hallways. No one paid any special attention to me, nor ignored me. It was all one seamless whole. When everyone gathers to practice, attention is on the meditations, visualizations, prayers, and mantras. Contemplation is on the perfection of the higher qualities of being—wisdom, generosity, insight, concentration, compassion, patience, perseverance, discipline, or renunciation. When all are gathered for the same purpose, everyone is too focused on realizing enlightenment for the benefit of all beings to be distracted by what anyone else was doing. So I blended in, one among the wizened old men and beautiful young women with moonlike faces. The entire day passed in puja. The shining light of the sacred temple hall generated a field that enveloped us all.

Before I knew it, it was late afternoon. The monks dispersed to their quarters and the mood around the monastery changed. Celebration was in the air. The villagers moved from the temple into a plateau jutting out from the cliffside about twenty minutes' walk down from the monastery. Wooden kegs of chang had been prepared and the dancing began. Beautiful circle dances were led by the women, their hands flowing in an arc, planting seeds and harvesting grain. They sang in high voices, their heads bowing with the steps, the jewels in their *perags* catching the late sunlight from the distant west. Then the men sang and danced, flowing in and out of the circle as they held the ends of their sashes, stomping and circling in step, old, young, and middle-aged. Children ran about like little sandpipers or snuggled into their mothers or fathers' lap. Teenagers eyed each other, boys and girls in the sparks of summer love. So many smiles. The feeling was indescribably easeful and happy.

A beautiful woman adopted me and took me back to her home. Her skin was milky white, soft like the moon, and luminous. She shone like the dakinis and her movements were just as fluid and magical. It was a long way from the party to her house, way back down and across the fields. The night was settling thickly around us as we arrived at her home. By this point, I'd learned enough Zanskari to converse a little, still we didn't talk much along the way, filled by the prayer festival and spent by the celebrations. There was a Hindu father and son also staying at her house for the night, traders buying crafts to take back and sell in Manali. She took me up to the open room on the roof where I slept deeply and peacefully.

I emerged from the cocoon of sleep, feeling clear and light. Different. Some metamorphosis seemed to have taken place, which I was part of but not privy to. It didn't matter what I knew or not. Everything was easy, smooth like the surface of a still lake. Not hurrying and not tarrying, I put my gear together, had a light breakfast of salt butter tea and flat breads and started walking northwards. There were passes to cross and distances to traverse. I was still some ways from my end point but Lingshet marked the beginning of decompression towards whatever my next chapter would be. As solid as my steps were on the path, inside I felt like I was floating, a little lighter, inexplicably happy, and free from shadow. Everything seemed clear, simple, purposeful. I had direction though I couldn't quite articulate what it was.

The puja had brought a lot of traders from adjacent towns and valleys to the monastery and the next day visitors scattered in all different directions. Each little party set about their own life's business. We'd dipped into the same blessing well and now shone with the same afterglow, carrying the imprints in our hearts, the *tsog* in our pockets, and the protection of the knotted red blessing cords around our wrists. A group of shepherds overtook me, one offered to carry my pack up to the first pass of the day.

What a good life, wandering at the top of the world. The passes had started to feel familiar. There were so many steep ascents and descents, ridges reaching up, followed by narrow scrambles over the tops. My eyes were learning to pick out the chortens in the distance, stuck to the highest passable dint in the mountains. With their prayer flags flapping in the wind, they looked like tethered falcons, waiting to be released. Recognizing the chortens in the distance was invaluable, they marked the places where the pass was easiest to cross and guided my steps from a long way away. The ritual blessings chanted at the top for safe passage helped ease my fears, too. There was intention imbued into the space. The practice at these spots, which I now followed too, is to leave a small stone on top, reciting the mantra of Chenrezig, the Buddha of Compassion.

Within a few hours, we reached Nietukse La, straddling the ridge at 3,570 meters. When I arrived at the chorten, I added my stone. Another mantra, another blessing in praise of the bodhisattvas. We started down together then I took my pack back as they traversed the ridge, following a different path to a high mountain hut where they'd graze their animals for some time. Even though I walked alone, I felt the mountains walking with me, their presence a warm companion, and the chattering of the wind against the rocks a happy conversation.

It was down and up again, over Kupa La and then my greatest challenge so far: Singi La with its intimidating 5,060 meters, 16,600 feet, without ropes, oxygen, cleats, or even boots. I found a place to camp so I'd be well rested and fed. Climbing that high would tax my systems and I was learning how to pace myself and prepare. I'd want to make it up and over by midday so I could shelter on the descent if I didn't make it all the way to the level ground. The night was easy. Ever since I'd crossed Hanumil La something had changed. Every new pass was still exciting, still a challenge, still a goal, yet that feeling that I *had* to make it, that it meant something about me, that something was missing without it no longer lurked in my veins. I still made effort, still pushed beyond exhaustion, still felt fear, but some *tanha* or craving had evaporated and even with the ups and downs, something stayed level, even.

The morning dawned clear and when the last stars faded into the turquoise sky, I packed my sleeping bag and the flatbreads I'd cooked for the climb and started, one foot in front of the other. The mountain face was austere, brown, and somewhat bleak, without flowers or snow to break up the face of the rock. Fortunately, the path was easily wide enough and I climbed at a steady incline. Each switchback rose and I could feel my lungs working hard. I slowed, allowing my body to settle and my heart to catch up. Hour after hour I rose. Nibbling my flatbreads, sipping water, watching the path, glancing up ahead. I was surprisingly calm, it was almost as if I were still walking the wide valley floor, something hadn't really moved.

Grasping or craving is one of the deadly fetters in Buddhism. Greed, anger, aversion, sloth, and torpor are all fetters, ensnaring us in our lower natures, winding us up in a tangle so we end up lashing out and creating negative karma, suffering for others and ultimately for ourselves. Grasping is subtle, I reflected as I climbed higher. Wanting the next peak or higher pass or the next teaching or longer retreat could either be of pure intention or tinged with tanha, wanting, needing, feeling incomplete without. This was not what I wanted my journey to be. It was not what I saw in the Zanskaris around me. Not what I felt in the Lamas and nuns.

The minutes and steps passed. My head felt light and it was getting harder and harder to will my legs to move. I was stopping to rest every fifty steps. Then every thirty steps. Then every twenty. The altitude can play tricks with your mind. And your own thoughts can play tricks with your mind too. I could feel how my mind was twisting non-grasping into a lack of will to go on. I couldn't go down and I no longer wanted to go up. Sometimes our will to live has a life of its own and, in this case, mine rose up with a vengeance. With all the pressure of everything I'd ever wanted to do, all the lofty goals I aspired to, and even all the trivial mundane things left undone in my young life, my will reared its head. Like an angry cobra ready to strike, I felt my it snaking up my spine, wriggling me forward with venom-like precision. I was going to move.

I was going to make it to the top. I was not going to cave in and retreat or sink into oblivion on the side of the mountain.

I gulped in the thin air and pushed my feet into the ground, one after another, one after another. A half hour later I was closer. A half hour after that I was closer still. One after another, one after another. I didn't really have any thoughts at this point. It was sheer will propelling me forward, consuming all the energy I had, with nothing left for thinking, vacillating, or especially not for retreating. Almost at the top, I could see the exultant prayer flags of the chorten. Jagged incisors of the mountain range spread out to the horizon line. A few more minutes, a few more minutes, a few last steps. I made it!

I had reached the pass I'd marveled at before heading out from Srinagar all those weeks ago. I had watched the deceptively small mark on my map draw nearer and nearer. Singi La, 5060 m. My heart pounding, I recited the prayers, balanced my small rock on top of another on the lid of the chorten, exhilarated. I felt that if I willed it, I could lift my arms and fly.

Among all reapings,
the autumn harvest is supreme.
Among all tracks,
the track of the elephant is supreme.
Among all ideas,
the idea of impermanence and death is supreme
Because with it, you eliminate
All attachment, ignorance, and pride.

THE BUDDHA
(5TH CENTURY BCE)

Chapter Sixteen
Equanimity & A Death

The next hours were a blur. Mountain passes are not a place to tarry, and I moved down quickly. Heading down is hard on the knees but far easier on the mind. No tricks of Mara thwarting the way. I could almost feel the air get thicker and richer though I think it was just the relief of heading down towards wider more level ground. There were some ups and downs, my mind so spent they hardly registered. The valley floor seemed to be rising up to meet me, as much as I was descending down to it. Somewhere in the middle, two passes, sometime after Skynpatta, the river and I met. It had taken all the rest of the hours of light to reach some level ground; time, space, and my body rippled in an altered state. I set up camp by a circle of rocks. Somehow in this degree of spentness, I managed to carry water, build a fire, fuel my body with salt tea and soy nuggets, rub out the knots in my tired calves, and finally stretch into the warmth and comfort of bed. Like cloud cover, a strange sleep descended over me, thick, misty, and dreamy without any clear forms.

When I awoke and started gathering myself for this next stretch, I felt an unfamiliar calm. The usual small mosquito itches of plans and things to accomplish had receded and the constant ticker of self-analysis and self-criticism had turned off. It was quiet on the Wall Street of my mind. I was used to making so much effort in meditation, it was so unfamiliar to let my mind be as it was. My gears had downshifted and while I was still running smooth and easy, I wasn't needing to spin so fast and chase so much. Breathing felt rich, drinking in the nutrients of the bright air. I ate, packed, and continued north. It looked like the way would be fairly easy for most of the day, level on a high valley floor.

I was enjoying the walk, a light green covered much of the valley, little plants brightening up the earth. The valley was happy, laughing in the way contours and shapes do sometimes. Late morning, I heard the tinkling of horse bells coming up from behind me. Two Zanskaris with three horses were catching up to me. Two horses were only lightly packed, and a third just held a blanket and light wooden saddle frame. We exchanged greetings and the familiar back and forth of wayfarers. Where are you heading? Where have you come from? What is your name? We found we were heading the same direction for the rest of the day. Karma and Yeshe were meeting a herder, where they'd leave two of the horses and continue on to Leh. They hoisted my pack onto the white pony with the empty saddle and we started walking. Karma chewed a stalk of lemony grass that rolled and bobbed like an unlit cigar, Yeshe, the more talkative of the two, walked next to me. I asked what I could and told what I could, then proceeded to learn the names of everything I could see in my surroundings. We laughed a lot, stopped for tea periodically, and the day felt as lighthearted as we were.

While we walked on wide flat ground, the path gradually rose higher and higher until the valley floor was a good five hundred meters above the river. There was plenty of room between us and the wall of mountains, maybe a half hour walk but the path skirted closer to the edge that dropped to the river. Yeshe and I walked ahead with one of the horses, while our grass nibbling friend followed up the rear with the white pony and the other small brown horse. Horses smell good, their tight muscles and short fur catch the light. The horse we walked with had colorful threads braided into its halter, and though dusty its mahogany-black coat gleamed. Horses have a presence. Not like people but they have their own being-ness. It was soothing to be with them. We kept moving, Yeshe singing songs under his breath. After some time had passed, we realized we seemed to have lost the other horse driver. My friend whistled low piercing whistles and calls that echoed down the canyon but Karma didn't answer. It was odd that he'd be so far behind us to be out of earshot, we were only moving at a moderate pace. No worry, was Yeshe's attitude. We stopped and propped our walking sticks against a boulder, waiting for him to catch up. It must have been just over an hour when Karma showed up small in the distance. It seemed like only one horse was following but I figured it must be my eyesight.

When he arrived, true enough, Karma only had one of the two horses he'd been walking with and he was carrying my pack on his back. I searched his face for clues as to what might have happened. Did he cross paths with a friend and pass on the white pony? Did he leave the horse to graze and decide to come back for him later? There didn't seem to be a problem, Karma's expression was calm and even. He was even smiling and shaking his head as he described to Yeshe what had happened. They talked a lot and I began to piece together the story.

It seemed the pony had spooked. All of a sudden, it broke into a gallop, heading straight to the edge of the cliff. The horse ran north along the edge, tossing his head and shaking, as if he wanted to free himself of a demon on his back. Karma whistled and called. He quickly secured the other horse's reins under a heavy boulder so he wouldn't follow and then shouted and clapped and walloped his thighs to break the horse's fright, all the while running as fast as he could. He ran but the horse was too far ahead and too wild. Then his hooves hit a soft part of the embankment. The ground gave way, crumbling over the edge. The horse slipped, flailed its legs, and tumbled over the cliff.

Karma, breathless, reached the spot, the horse had met a quick and painless end on a rocky outcrop not too far down the slope. The river steamed another few hundred meters below, it was fortunate the ledge had broken the horse's fall. Karma climbed down the side of the embankment. He stroked the top of the horse's head, reciting mantras, allowing the horse's life essence to settle, allowing the fear to dissipate, reminding the horse of what a faithful servant he had been, how many sacks of tsampa he had carried to the monasteries for great pujas, how many Rinpoches he had travelled with. In this way, he helped guide the horse's consciousness into the bardo, the inbetween state between one life and the next, with the mantras and good deeds to calm and carry his spirit through so it could find its way to a better rebirth, one where it could hear and practice the dharma, and keep moving on the path towards enlightenment.

When it felt like the disturbance had settled, Karma untied my pack and the saddle, lifted the blankets, and carried it all on his back up the side of the hill back to the valley floor. He packed some on the brown pony's back but took my rucksack on his own.

As he finished recounting his story, Yeshe, who'd been making a fire and heating tea the whole time, filled his cup, poured some dried yak cheese into his friend's hand, and shook his head back and forth.

"We are all going to die one day. We never know when. We think it might be too soon. But we die at just the right time. We must always be ready, it is the way of things. It is so, the wheel of birth and death, the wheel of becoming. That's why we must practice the dharma, so when the time comes there will be no grasping or fear and we can stay calm through the great terror of the bardo and direct our rebirth into a beneficial realm."

Karma nodded his head, blew on his steaming tea, and chewed the nuggets of dried cheese. This was the way of things.

Was it somehow my fault? I worried. Was it the foreign smell of my pack that spooked the horse? I tried to express my concern and regret and offer to compensate them for the horse. I don't know if they fully understood me, but they just kept shaking their heads no. Their equanimity was so complete, they seemed to embrace this turn of events as day embraces night. They had already moved on.

After all the lost time, Yeshe explained that they needed to travel more quickly to reach their destination before nightfall. I thanked them and took my pack. They quickly disappeared into the distance ahead of me and were soon out of sight.

I slowed down and when I found a good place to camp for the night in a wide part of the valley, I stopped. Though it was colder here than against the mountainside, I was able to watch the great dome of stars overhead and reflect on the day.

The horseman's equanimity was so genuine it was as if there was no other way to react. For me, all the examples of loss I'd seen in my culture, a car dinging someone else's fender, a plate slipping out of a hand and shattering on the floor, a friend moving away from the neighborhood were accompanied with intense emotion. Anger, frustration, denial sadness, or regret. For Karma and Yeshe, there really weren't any emotional disturbances. Neither swore, complained, insisted it be otherwise, or blamed me. I felt it must have been my foreign smell that startled the horse but since they weren't sure, they didn't assume to know what they didn't know. That animal must have been a big part of their wealth and livelihood. But as is part of the magic and the depth of practice in this valley, they accepted life, death, fortune, and misfortune equally and continued on.

Finally, I fell asleep under the midnight blue.

In my sleep I must have kept processing that sense of the precariousness and immediacy of life and death. In the west, I had hardly encountered anyone or anything that had died, except my grandfather when I stayed by his hospital bed, putting together puzzles in the waiting room, as he slipped away to cancer. It was just me and my mother, my grandmother too, though I don't remember her presence that well. Aside from that single incident I had always been shielded. Death was spoken about in hushed tones. Hidden behind hospital walls or disappeared, like my pet goldfish, finches, and parade of little white mice with red eyes I named Twinkletoes. They all vanished when they became that mysterious word "dead."

Being around death used to rock me. Not because I'm afraid of death; I believe in the continuation of life or consciousness in some way, maybe not so linearly as the Tibetans, but in the sense that the life force continues and has momentum, a single life merging back into the pool of consciousness to eventually form into a new being. It rocked me to think about death because I didn't know how to think about it. Even though it was ubiquitous, it seemed so foreign. And that seemed strange. Prince Siddhartha was shielded from old age, sickness, and death. It was a rude awakening when he left the palace and encountered each human stage in turn. He realized however rich, however pampered and protected, there was no escaping aging, illness, and end of this life's incarnation. In the postmodern Western world, we are all like the Prince in so many ways. Wealthy, pampered, shielded. Anesthetized against life. Without seeing the cosmic order, we lose the tangible knowing that we are part of a continuum. That continuum fuels our human care.

Here in the valley, there is balance. The continuum of life is natural and each of the stages of manifestation and dissolution holds its own place. The rhythms of the seasons, the amount each field can yield, the times for prayer and puja, and the space for community and togetherness all flow in an out of each other, like the tides of life rising and falling. Without that denial of what is sure to come, life feels more easy, more immediate, more full. The Zanskari horseman's acceptance of the fate of his white pony spoke volumes. His equanimity an attainment I now strove for. I had no idea I was so bound by denial and fear until I encountered what it could be to accept what is and be free.

The root and foundation of the Great Way
is said to be the will to achieve highest enlightenment
in order to benefit the countless living beings.

Make every effort to generate this thought
and to transcend its opposite, the self-cherishing mind.

As all things that exist are interdependent,
All things thus are by nature void.

Cultivate this vision;
and be aware of the world as illusory,
like a magician's creation.

GENDUN GYATSO PALZANGPO
THE SECOND DALAI LAMA
(1475-1542)

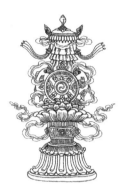

Chapter Seventeen
Freedom and Education

The next day was steady. I continued to move north on a gradual incline. I walked through the light of the morning to see the next marker way ahead, the base of another high pass. Two Ladakhi men came up on the path behind me, one with a beautiful white horse and one with a huge yak bull. The bull breathed heavily, mist coming out of his nostrils and moistening the shaggy wool around his neck. He smelled sweet and musty, a smell that soothed me. The large apricots of his eyes were soft and deep. His hooves were huge, larger twice my outstretched hand. In spite of his girth, he carried himself with grace. I wouldn't want to get on the wrong side of him on a bad day but standing near him was oddly calming. A protector. The Ladakhis and I exchanged a few words and we continued on together. Animals and humans, we were different and we were a continuum of complexity and consciousness. We were the same in our embeddedness on the wheel of existence. A gentle protectorship traveled both ways between us.

As the afternoon shadows lengthened, I stopped for the night and yak bull and his small party continued on. I found a good camp within reach of the base of the climb to the next pass. Though the mountains towered, massive and indifferent, finding a resting spot in their foothills was less intimidating, more like snuggling into their lap. I lay down, the purple shadow of the mountains blanketing me. Here I didn't feel alone. Here, the mountains, the sense of place, and the connections of the day kept me company, a room in my heart full of friends. I lay on the ground, listening to the earth shift in its sleep. There was a magnificent full moon. I lifted my hand to watch its moonshadow on the ground. She seems to stay full for days up here, so close and so much bigger as she rests atop the silhouette of the hills in her climb to the black sky. I am tired and full. It is so good to be here. The mountains are beyond description.

I fell asleep thinking about the education I received growing up. How little it prepared me for life with a big L. I learned history without learning how to question the assumptions, who was deciding what was right, what was good, what was progress? We didn't learn ethics or a philosophy of freedom until college, that wonderful twelve-person seminar where, under the penetrating intellect of Dick Polenberg we debated Supreme Court cases on Civil Liberties and Civil Disobedience from both sides. Each student took a case. I argued the case about whether the Hare Krishna cult had the right to preach their gospel in public places like airports. An actual case. Not so easy in its details. As a young child, I had encountered a couple of shaven-headed saffron-clad Krishna's pushing flowers into passerby's hands outside my favorite children's shoe store. I remember wondering why the adults, including my mother, were so frightened by them. What is freedom? If your freedom impinges on another, how do you decide? What goes in the name of freedom? What are the structures of culture that support freedom? What does freedom require of us? What is required in a society to support freedom?

I was still thinking about these things. I had always thought about questions like that, for those who hadn't, I figured college is far too late in life to begin. By that age, we've already concretized so many beliefs that mold our views, open-ended inquiry becomes difficult. We then have to find the courage to re-learn, to question our own worldview. In my family, my father being a particle physicist and my brother in engineering physics, the dominant perspective was scientific materialism. What you could see and measure was valued as true, real, definable. Our human responses were seen as unreal or unreliable because we could not measure or accurately reproduce them. They were malleable, mercurial. In my family, the "soft sciences" were a reluctantly accepted lesser cousin to the hard or true sciences. Spirituality was even that much lower on the list. My brother frequently told me that I wasn't as smart as him, because even though we went to the same university, and I took upper-level classes in my first year and achieved the same grades as he, I was in Humanities and he was in Engineering Sciences. As he liked to tell me "everyone knows the Arts are easy." The implication being, those domains are not valuable or worthwhile for serious people. That scientific bias tried to steer me away from contemplations about freedom and from my effort to understand the structures of culture that would facilitate our higher potentials, rather than what we have now, cultural structures that are eroding our experience of wellbeing and the wellbeing of the planet on which we all live.

As I matured, I started to see how much the scientists in my family took on faith, how many of their experiments rested on theory and abstraction, which I figured is sort of like faith. I thought more about experiments like the double-slit light experiment, which showed that the intention of the observer watching the experiment influenced whether light would show up as a wave or a particle. Wild. How could light know? What does that mean about sentience? Consciousness? Interconnectivity? And why, if we're supposed to be getting smarter, figuring out quarks and mesons, do people in my home culture seem more fearful, more angry, more displaced, and more deeply unhappy?

When we think about education or the pursuit of knowledge, our first question needs to be, "What are we educating for? How vital are harmony, contentment, joy, actualization, and freedom to our educational goals?" What we're aiming for reveals the underpinnings of everything we teach.

Context shapes our worldview. Our worldview shapes how we act, what we value and what we discount.

Here in Zanskar, I felt the difference in values among the simplest things and the emphasis of learning about the impact of our own actions on everything around us. As sparse as the material life was, the cultivation of higher human potentials was beyond abundant. In many ways to me, the humanity here felt far more evolved than my Western world where blame, frustration, and desire is inbred. It seemed to me that our system, almost intentionally if albeit mostly unconsciously, fostered avoiding the laws of cause and effect. The result? An increasingly dysregulated population.

The next day, I began to walk early. It was going to be a long day to get up and over Sirsir La. On the way, I crossed a lower pass. The snow had slid down the mountainside, covering the path. It was many feet thick, unstable, and dangerous. I had to find a way to cross the river to get to the left bank and find a new track up and over the pass. Fortunately, around midday, I met up with the men with the yak bull again and they agreed to take my pack for twenty rupees. The two men had earrings as thick as rings and I liked them. The timing couldn't have been better. I enjoyed being able to look around and walk lighter and the way was steep. I was heading north, and the end of the valley would not be that many days off once I crossed these 4,990 meters.

In early afternoon, we crossed a short pass near Photoksar. It was a quick, steep ascent to 4,200 meters, tracing a skinny path over the ridge with high peaks encircling us as far as I could see, an ocean of magnificence, before we headed down again to the river. We walked along the western bank above the fields until we came to a bridge and we could cross to the east side again.

They kept going, not at all tired, while I rested in the strong sun for a brief spell. I stood up again and continued to skirt the corner of the mountain's base. I was tired, deeply tired. It felt like a magnet was pulling all the energy out of my legs. Every step took more and gave less. The Ladakhis were long out of sight and I had to keep going to meet up with them as they had everything I owned with them. I willed them to stop and wait, see that I wasn't strong like them. But they were far ahead. No sign of them, they clearly hadn't stopped so neither could I. With each breath I pushed myself forward. Moving through the quicksand of exhaustion, the force of inertia pushed back on me with intensity. I could hardly make my thighs move. I let my mind go still, flatlined the physical strain. Although tired to my core, in an unfamiliar way, the slippery slope of discouragement and despair didn't take over that still space. Letting my mind go quiet, without concluding that that meant I was giving up, revealed another dimension. The immediate present. No future. No measuring. No "how long will this take?" No blame, no disparagement. Just the minute immediacy, just what was right in front of me. Time passed, all the while seeming to stand still. Distance passed, without one step seeming any further or different than the one before.

After a long while, I caught up to the two men and the yak bull. They were laughing and telling stories, fresh and steady as they had been when we first met up. My senses drank in their good cheer. The yak breathed his heavy presence, shifting his weight, standing on watch, reassuring. I reached into my pack and pulled out some bread I'd made a few nights earlier. The fire-baked rotis kept for days and were easy to grab. It was my first more substantial meal since supper the night before. When they saw I had finished, they packed up, still laughing and jostling each other. I didn't think I could even stand let alone walk. My bones felt at the same time light and so heavy, weighted and weak. But I felt I needed to stay with them, the pass was too much on my own. I followed. They were intent to cross over Sirsir La at 4,990 meters. When something is non-negotiable, and you let the mind fall into submission, amazing things are possible.

The way up was an extraordinary climb. I hardly could watch the surroundings. I imagined invisible ropes around my waist, hoisting me up one hard won step after another. I anchored my gaze on the top ridge, single pointed, like the meditations I had learned from a book as a teenager, focusing on a candle flame with soft unmoving gaze. The practice worked even here, moving me from effort into stillness and out of time. The sky was clear. The air dry. The wind slight. In this meditation in motion, everything moved as liquid, climbing up was not so much as a foreign body on a rock ridge, but as a scene on a single canvas, white cloud, blue sky, sienna rock, pale girl all one whole.

In the end, the pass itself was not so hard to cross. Once up and over, it was downhill for a long way. The two men sang and hollered, their day a happy one, always a happy one, for no reason other than it was today. We started coming to level ground and I started noticing some good camping spots close to the river.

I parted ways with the traders, loving that big yak bull as he heaved his heavy body away from where I stood. Why do we sometimes connect with individual animals? Why do some feel magical, powerful, awake? When I look at his lumbering hind quarters, he seems every bit an animal as any other bull. The Tibetans say the animal rebirth is much lower than the human realm because they are dull and can't contemplate the dharma and what it means to awaken. Mostly animals feel that way to me and then there will be one that for whatever reason stands out from the herd and has a presence that communicates something more than their consciousness is supposed to be able to do, like a little communication chute connecting my consciousness to theirs, bypassing my mind. I said some mantras over this one for a good rebirth, for freedom from suffering, sending him appreciation and blessing for his presence and for whatever it was that transpired between us during this time. As a meditated on him I could all but feel his wiry fur in my fingers and smell his musty oil.

I choose a lovely spot on the right bank of a feeder stream. I set a fire circle up near a narrow wooden bridge with a welcoming low stone mani wall. I was not far from Hanupatta Gompa and I imagined many pilgrims, monks, and lamas had walked this way before me. I circumambulated the spot, chanting mantras along the way. I loved these walls, sprouting up in the middle of nowhere, prayer anchors, reminding you of what was important, and where to rest your consciousness. When you come upon a mani wall, you always walk clockwise, with your right shoulder to the wall, reminding you of intentionality even in the middle of the wilderness with no one watching. The beautiful chiseled rocks with text, mantras, and ornate Buddhas were created with intention, left out in the elements to spread their blessings, equally over everything, sanctifying the space.

I looked around at this little indent in the valley. Though I had revived some with the energy of the descent, it was beyond time to rest. I laid out my ground cloth, tattered Thinsulite pad, and sleeping bag, ready for the night to come. I could hardly believe I had made it, seven hours walking. The Ladakhis had pushed me far beyond my limits. I could feel strength from that, even in my spent state. Everything was part of the path to awakening. I was grateful. In the early twilight, I sipped some of the bitter Ladakhi tea that they'd poured into my canteen before we parted. Somehow, they seemed to have known everything, without appearing to take notice of me or anything in particular at all.

Having given up all other intentions,
Being motivated by only one thought,
I shall strive to settle my mind in equipoise
By means of calm abiding
And to subdue it
With superior insight.

SHANTIDEVA
(7TH—8TH CENTURY CE)

Chapter Eighteen
Decompressing

The days and kilometers were taking me closer and closer to the close of this journey. Crossing Photaksar was a demarcation line and I had mixed feelings. I was nearing the northern edge of the Zanskari valley where the footpaths connect with the road, a road that connects West to East, Srinagar to Leh. As much as I loved being in the valley, I was also ready to walk out of the wandering wilderness. It felt time to move on, time for a next phase. These almost forty days taught me much and stretched me in many ways, my inner elastic had changed shape and I wanted to see how. It felt like I'd gone as far as I could on my own, at least at this stage. I was ready to see more people and process in my own language, exchange with those who shared a similar background, who had similar questions but different insights, where together in our awkward westernness, I wouldn't feel so clumsy and uninformed.

It takes commitment to be so solitary, it takes purpose to keep the mind on track and have it not veer too far in a cul-de-sac of angst, self-doubt, or discouragement. Purpose draws you towards it like a lode star or magnet, and without a clear enough line of sight, the austerity becomes overwhelming. I had pretty much done what I set out to do and it had taken me beyond anything I could have imagined. The sense of being ready to exit the valley starting building in me. I may come back for a much longer stretch, to retreat, but I wasn't ready for that yet. For now, I had fulfilled my purpose.

On the mundane plane, I had to admit I was getting tired of tsampa and salt butter tea, and tired of so much time just with my own mind. Aloneness seems easy, no frictions, no compromises, but it takes strength from the soul to bear with it, day after day. The rocks and eagles were company, and the scattered wayfarers that I met helped, but it was different than living in community. In long meditation retreats, I always felt the benefit of the structure and silent companionship; as alone as I was sitting with my own mind in the dense silence, at least I knew what I were supposed to be doing, hour by hour. I sat zabuton to zabuton with other people who were equally struggling through the maze of their own thoughts. The vast open sky was another thing entirely. Clear light. Unobstructed seeing. No guardrails, no guidance to set the goals, no new food for contemplation. No corrections. No one to give me antidotes to the poison of my own obscurations. I had the feeling I was learning and like a toddler's teetering steps, I was accumulating my share of spiritual scratched knees along the way.

I didn't pass anyone on the trail that day. I walked by a few people working in the fields outside of Photoksar. Backs bent, heads down, singing, they had their dharma to do. Hoe and water, prune and weed. I realized the last conversation I had had in my language was days ago, sometime before Lingshet with a French family with two children. They were walking with a guide and had set out their mid-morning snack. Their porter brewed sugar milk tea with Horlick's milk powder on a kerosine stove and spread out coconut biscuits, plain water crackers and Amul cheese triangles, individually wrapped in their tin foil. They invited me and I sat with them for a short while, noticing how they nibbled and discarded half-eaten cheese and cookies, tossing out half-drunk tea. When you have so much, it's hard to appreciate it each time. When you have little, every small nourishment in life tastes so much richer. We can't really help it in the West, we're acculturated into abundance, swimming in excess, and breathing in the air of wanting. As much as I critiqued it, it was my culture and it was time to re-enter. I could feel the magnet of the end pulling on me. But there were still several more passes to cross and some days to go.

In the morning, I felt nervous ants walking in my mind. I clicked off at a fast pace, singing to keep myself going. At Hanupatta, a small village of a dozen and a half houses, and a tiny gompa, I stopped for tea. While I was resting at the side of the path at the edge of the village, an unexpected party arrived from a side path. My friends with the yak bull had met up with Roger and another horsemen and they were all walking and laughing, joking and singing. They joined me and pulled out their pot to boil more tea. We sat together, Roger and I catching up on our journeys, what was hard, what was easy, where we were heading. It was nice to share our adventures and excitement. He seemed content with how his path had turned out and I with mine. He was going to stay in this little village for a few more days before exiting the valley to use up all his vacation time before he needed to fly home. The horsemen had business in town. When it was time, I packed up and continued ahead on my own.

The narrow green valley smelled good. Just keep moving, I thought to myself. But now that I was nearing the end of this chapter, those nagging questions came back. What was my actual goal? There was no motivation to do anything extraordinary without clarity around purpose. I could be anywhere. The gears of my mind creaked and clanked. Like a good mechanic knows when to tune an engine before problems develop, I was learning to tune my mind towards more useful directions when it started to show signs of malfunction.

Dedicating merit or the fruits of generous actions and accomplishments helps turn the mind towards others in a way that enriches rather than depletes. I'd learned that in theory on retreat and over these weeks struggling with my mind, I'd learned it in actuality by watching others. To tune up my thoughts, I started dedicating any merit that might have been accumulated from the meditation I'd done over this time, from the rituals I'd been part of, from the chortens I'd passed, and the mani walls I'd circumambulated.

I had proven to myself that I wasn't just a city girl so divorced from the rhythms of the land that I couldn't fend for myself without technology. I didn't need a refrigerator or food wrapped in plastic and shipped thousands of miles. I didn't need electricity to cook or pipes to shower. It was a basic life and I felt the stronger for immersing myself in it. I had met the challenges of high passes, one after the other, from 3,500 meters all the way up to 5,060 meters. I had watched, learned, and followed the rhythms of the people who had lived like this for generations, and it had changed me. I was grateful for what I'd carried, how much each of these treasures had supported me: my tattered Indian army map showing me the contours of the mountains and small dotted lines for footpaths, my little vocabulary of Hindi, Urdu, and Tibetan, a cooking pot and cup, matches and candle ends. I had walked through discouraging thoughts, through fearful feelings, and bone-tired muscles. I'd stayed on track, stayed in the light. The hills had shown me the riches of sleeping under the jewels of billions of stars. The cleverness of the Zanskaris showed me how housing animals on the first floor to keep the living spaces warm. The rinpoches had chanted over me and revealed how the way to higher consciousness take time and infinite patience, and is felt in the fraction of a moment with a smile. The children showed me what love, security, and responsibility do, and how regal the right kind of pride sits on their shoulders. I kept dedicating merit, and in the process realized how phenomenally rich I'd become. I had so much to give back.

I came to a cave in a very narrow rock canyon. The shadows of the mountainside were striped red, green, and purple with different layers of sediments, different eras of existence. The tips of the mountains were tooth-jagged. The way ahead led over a pass but I had lost the trail. I needed to cross the river but wasn't sure where the bridge was. It was getting to be early afternoon, the wind was picking up, and I felt unsure of moving forward. I took a nervous nap in a little cave, waiting for another wayfarer to pass so I could cross with them. I felt certain someone would come, as the mouth of the valley neared with it the road en route to Leh. More and more people would be crossing this way, I could wait.

It wasn't long before a couple of figures came towards me heading direction Wanla. They stopped for tea, the ritual I was now accustomed to. We shared breads and we walked on together. They were mischievous with each other, filled with vim and vigor as the Indian billboards liked to say. One was an elder monk, the other a horseman, both in fine spirits and intent on getting me to laugh. The monk kept asking if I had a camera. Finally I reluctantly pulled it out of my pack, and they had a great time taking photos of me, of us together, and of the horses. He was naturally camera ready, with charming faces and fun in his eyes. He wore a big green leaf atop under his tulip-shaped maroon silk hat. It kept his sweating shaved head cool.

At one point, the path narrowed with a steep drop on one side and we stopped to unload the horses, carrying our gear until it widened again. The horses were nimble but, as I had seen, could slip, and there was not much we could do to rescue them if they fell. Once the trail widened again and moved away from the cliff, we loaded the horses with our gear. The land just before Wanla changed again. Instead of boldly striped rocks, the valley widened and became lush and green. It was later in the summer than when I had started and the crops were doing well. The grains had shot up, now taller than I. It was warm all afternoon with a mild wind, just enough to dry our sweat and keep a smile on our faces. This part of the valley got good sun and I was drinking in the warmth inside and out. We camped by the river. It rained a bit during the night. A straw mouse scratching to get inside my sleeping bag and the horses chewing just behind my head kept me partially awake, and happy.

My companions set out early in the morning. I took my time, savoring my final sections of the trail. I walked along the river to the bridge then continued up a canyon that smelled cool and sweet from a short light rain. It was perfectly silent in the canyon; I couldn't even hear the calls of the birds. The ground dried out as I existed the canyon and there were small green desert plants adding a dusting of color to the sandy ground. The other side of a low pass was an easy descent to a tiny town, perched on a little hill. I could feel the nearness of modern civilization even though I couldn't see it yet.

The final village I walked through was circled by green fields. Houses built in layers lined the hillside. From a distance, it looked like they were perched precariously one on top of the other but once I arrived I found they all were much more spacious, with big verandas bedecked with brightly colored prayer flags and pipes with running water leading into the courtyards. The townspeople were wearing a mixture of kurta pyjamas, Western running pants and t-shirts, and Tibetan overcoats. I could feel the mix of the old and the new, like the way the water changes color in a river delta, the water striated by currents and sand as one stream enters a bigger body of water. In this case, the small stream of Zanskari culture blended with the Indian road workers, soldiers, and global companies looking to capture new markets. Although the people in the valley may not have realized it yet, the shadow in my heart knew that life here would not be the same for much longer.

*The bodhisattva never indulges
in imagining that full enlightenment
can only occur in the distant future,
for every single thought flash reveals
the absence of limits, separation, and distance.*

PRAJNAPARAMITA SUTRAS
(100 BCE – 500 CE)

Chapter Nineteen
Inbetween Here & Eternity

Finally, I arrived. Lamayuru. The high and sacred town. The northeastern mouth of the Zanskar Valley. My journey through these hills had come to an end. I'd arrived at my destination, or at least at this stop on this part of my journey to awakening. The village of Lamayuru was set a little ways back from the road where I stood unsteadily, somewhat shocked. I moved as if in a dream, like through a wall of water. This was my destination, I reminded myself. I'd willed myself here, pushed through resistance and exhaustion, hit highs and thudded down low, saw magic and miracles on practically a daily basis. And, now what? A little sad, a little unsure, a little excited and very tired, I tried to take it in. This was my victory circle. I looked around me, still stunned.

Everything was open, wide open. I was looking ahead. My hands were as empty as a sackful of snow left out in the hot sun. There was nothing I could hold onto and take out of this valley. I was lighter than when I first came in. I wanted something to clutch, quantify. Tangibles eluded me. When you are changed by something it is no longer outside of you. Like the cup of merit emptied into the ocean, I had both nothing and was swimming in a sea of riches. My heart, stretched wide, had grown new muscles of care. Right now, it was pumping noisily, making itself known with a full and unfamiliar ache, not from attachment in the face of moving on, but from connection beyond time. The valley and her people had pulled me in, touched me with their quiet joy and rough happiness, melting so many subterranean ice walls in my being.

So much had happened and this moment, the close to the journey, loomed so large but oddly inconsequential. It was hard to know how I felt. Zanskaris have a custom of not saying goodbye. They just keep walking or step out of the door. Life is a flow, one moment into the next, meetings and partings, always meetings and partings. In my own awkward way, I was feeling there was nothing needed to mark this end. While there was a big lump in my throat and a stone in my heart, this parting was not as real as it might seem. The valley would continue to live in me, merged with my own karmic continuum, for as long as that momentum continued on. The people and the mountains I loved become honored through action, through my own intention to embody the dharma we shared.

There are no hard endings and beginnings between the manifest world and the eternity of that which was never born. Form and emptiness. Emptiness and form. The magic of Zanskar. The world outside. Seeking and realizing transcend place and even time as we know it. Carrying the intention to be liberated from location to location, from lifetime to lifetime, following rituals or no distinct form, all the while chopping wood, carrying water, never losing sight of the goal and the immediacy of its attainment.

I felt like I'd finally worn a pair of new boots that had been sitting in my closet forever. Once you lace up the pair and walk a few hundred kilometers, they shape around your foot. They become you through your imprint and you, through your efforts and memories, become them. While crossing this valley, I had imprinted myself into the shoe of my life. I'd made it fit me, and me alone. I still didn't know where I would go next or what I would do. But, for now, the way was open, free.

I stepped back from the road clumsily. From weeks of knowing the next step to so much unsurety, I also didn't know who I was supposed to be as I moved into a world that objectively was more familiar but which now seemed more foreign, more of an odd dream than some of the strangest sights I'd seen along the way. By the roadside, in the shade of the tourist restaurant, I noticed how much harder it was to tell the passing of time by the quality of the shadows and the light. It was harder to hear the rumble, the low chanting of the mountains. Harder to see the small movements of little animals and wide-winged birds as their shadows drew patterns on the canvas of the high peaks and deep valleys. I felt oddly constricted in my chest, a little blurry in my eyes. I looked down, all of the sudden self-conscious of my battered shoes and dusty hair. My grey Kashmiri pheran, which had kept me both warm and cool, and covered me when I had to relieve myself, now felt ill-fitting and a little embarrassing.

I set my pack against the side of a bench and waited for the next bus to come. The bitter diesel smell floated towards me from the asphalt road. The pockmarked guardrails of poured cement teetered by the gravel edge. The modern world felt cold and jagged, empty of the life and breath that animated the big mountain walls. I breathed and blinked, looking around, taking it all in, not comprehending. Moving forward anyway. Without ceremony, my adventure in Zanskar was coming to a close. My world was changing, like in *The Lion, The Witch, and the Wardrobe,* with one step I was striding through the door into another universe. Everything was re-orienting, but not gradually, more like a naked bulb flicked on in a bare room.

I started feeling like a walk-in in my own body. Confused, I moved inside the restaurant and picked up a menu. Finger-stained and creased, it listed traditional Indian-English fare: butter jam toast, milk tea, vegetarian cutlets, omelet, curried vegetables, fried rice, chappati. The kitchen seemed empty and forlorn. I couldn't bring myself to break my fast of local food and celebrate the end of my trek there. I ordered a chai and sat at a table on the dusty veranda, my first table and chair since the sweet days at Moti and Krishna's in Padum. I looked down the road into the distance and remembered the people who'd shared themselves and their homes with me.

I loved the quality of purity that I felt from these people. The simplicity and fullness. They wore the same pattern cloth from childhood to old age, generation after generation, yet their eyes were clear and bright with spontaneity. They tilled the same small plot of land, sowed the same crop rotation, and used the same tools, century after century. When it was harvest time, they heaved great loads of grass to the roof to dry. When it was planting time, they tilled and irrigated and sowed the seeds they'd kept. They recited the same prayers every day with commitment and devotion, faith, and love. They had freedom from useless deliberations and choices that led nowhere but to the tangled mass of the mind. Which television show? Which salad dressing? Which hairstyle Which car? Which spouse? Which country? To what end? They were free from highways that led fast, but to where? They had no apartment buildings with blank windows staring outward through uniform expressionless eyes. They rarely strayed from the rhythm of their culture, yet their spirits burst out through smiles so spontaneous and wide. They were so alive, free. From as soon as they could walk, they adventured. They watched endlessly captivating shifts of rock, sky, river, and shadow. They took in the brilliance of virgin snowfields, gleaming like a field of diamonds at sunrise. At the top of the world, they caught the sun's first rays before the light filtered down to kiss awake the lowlands.

Acclimatization is uncomfortable. Unmoored from structure, trying to figure out the next foothold of my path, I mostly felt unsure. What is allowing? What burns off the haze of past karma? What is the natural unfolding? What is the choice made out of fear or egotism? Doesn't every infatuation turn to ashes? Every flame flicker and die? Is there that which is unchanging? If there is, what created it? What was there before eternity? What is the beginning of the infinite? What extends past its end? How do I lift myself up so I can look down on the maze of existence, and see with laser-like clarity like the eagles do? Did the mountains have more to tell me?

Surfacing from the depths, I was re-entering a familiar atmosphere but the pressure change was still a shock to my system. The promise of more material ease reassured me. The questions about what I would do with my material freedom were a little harder. Sometimes the easiest way to look ahead is to look back, so I did, searching for patterns that would carry me forward.

When I was little, postcards had always left me with an odd sense of wanting. My father would send pictures of the alps from Cern, I just wanted to be inside the white and grey mountains. I was the kind of curious child that wanted to taste Pooh bear's honey in my own mouth, scramble around the tree roots in the forests and climb over ancient stone ruins, I liked to unearth surprise fungi and test them with my senses. As a teenager I wanted to know why the world was so harsh-edged and did it really need to be, what was missing? How do we bring it back? As a young adult, I began to follow the intimations of another track towards meaning and purpose. I read philosophy and poetry, talked to people who were returning from their own quest. My seeking led me all over, from gardening in an immigrant town in the Galilee to the late nights in the college library by the rushing gorges in Ithaca, to bumping along in boxcars crossing the great plains, to heaving heavy clamps on oil rigs in the baren east of Wyoming, to a summer job on a strawberry farm in the hippie town of Madison, all the way to the Copper Valley. I followed breadcrumb to breadcrumb, my signposts disappearing behind me. I had a path, it was just drawn with invisible ink, by an invisible hand. The texts say if we are sincere, the way will be revealed. I always seemed to find my way, though I was often unsure, I was never lost. There was a restlessness and a hunger in me. Maybe from past lives wasted or cut short of their potential, I viscerally felt how easily an entire life could pass. Something gnawed at me, something important, something I couldn't really grasp, yet I knew it was yet to be done.

I had come to a point where the pressure from within demanded a more intentional response and it drew me to the land of the yogis and the snow, where I could soak in the practice of each day, as fully as I could, bringing the mind of awakening into the forefront with meditation, teachings, study, retreat. Arriving on this continent, I stumbled on practices about the ephemeral nature of life and the inevitability of death. They stoke the fires of urgency and clear away the entangling brush of insignificant concerns. In Varanasi, I had sat with the Hindus by the burning ghats at the banks of the Ganga. I meditated amidst the smoke and reality of the rough end we will all eventually come to. On hot and dusty trains, in chai shops, and on retreat, I read texts describing how the Buddha sent his renunciates to meditate in the graveyard, visualizing lusted-after ones deteriorating, step by step, in the march of old age, sickness, and death. There was calm in the middle of that practice, it stilled the grasping mind.

When I set out for Zanskar, I'd told people I wanted to see the high mountains. I told myself that too. But the urgency with which I had to come here, that plucked me out of the dull haze of hippies in Srinagar was more than the mountains. It was what was hidden in the wrinkles of the land and the flotsam of the rivers. It was the intricate pathways roughed out by mantra and meditation. It was the time warp. Not just life as it had been, but life as it could be, a hidden *beyul* in existence amongst our regular life. Being here, in a valley shaped by the contours of enlightenment, there was time to enter into the contemplation beyond time. That space allows the doors of illumination to open. It could happen after decades of practice, or in an instant. No one can know the intricacies of our own karmic continuum. Never underestimate how close it might be or how quickly many more rounds of existence could be squandered.

My adventure in Zanskar was always intended to more than a journey of steps. As I walked, I found out what it was going to be. I walked off bad memories and discouraging habits of mind. I created distance between my own true aspiration in this life and the expectations of my culture. I stumbled and was guided.

What I was seeking, also pursued me. We stomach bumped, more than once, in ephemeral moments. That touch left me transfigured. I realized my error of seeking for more and greater experiences, in a flash the illusion of grasping splintered and shattered. I could never go back to the way I was before, once known, I knew that I'd known, even if I forget, I still know. Paradoxically, now knowing that no experience could ever change that which Is, it also revealed what a long way I had to go.

I had my whole life to live, the question was how to continue. Like the side of a cliff tells a geologist a billion-year story of experiences and formation, life in all its layers tells the story of the great dharma of impermanence, oneness, and love. It's a story that is unfolding and that we unfold with our own choices and intentions, karma and discernment. The texts say you must discover the truth yourself. They also say you must seek a living Buddha. Freedom is prior to structure. Truth is a pathless land. There are those who emanate wisdom. Their presence gives guidance and faith. Walking in the valley, I met masters in the wise ones, the lamas, the practitioners, and in the earth, sky, water, rock. I felt the currents of the unseen bodhisattvas, in all their myriad forms, blessing, guiding, maintaining a pulsating heaven in some subtle dimension of our consciousness.

I looked around me at the restaurant at the mouth of this special place, drinking the air and nestling into the vista through my sight. A knife-like pain shot through my heart. Light flashed behind my eyes, bright as the stream of all the stars I'd seen each night in the Milky Way. Unbidden, my heart folded over, bowed before the mystery and miracle of that which always is.

The enlightened art of the bodhisattva
is to appear to move in the transparent sphere
of conventional characteristics
and harmoniously functioning causality,
while remaining totally awake to the signlessness
and causelessness of sheer Reality.

PRAJNAPARAMITA SUTRAS
(100 BCE – 500 CE)

Chapter Twenty
An End, a Beginning, Beyond Time

Riding on a bus after a long time just walking was a discon-
certing experience. The diesel fumes coated the back of my
throat. They tasted bad, not like sweet horse or smoky wet
wool. The scenery went by so quickly; I crossed the land but
with no contact. It felt wrong. Disrespectful. Not honoring.
How could anyone feel anything but empty and aching riding
a Greyhound, all gone to search for America?

    I arrived in Leh some hours later, the long ride
bouncing through the deep, narrow canyon. Leh felt more
like a high desert, light brown and dry. We had passed several truck accidents; the roads were narrow and everyone
drove too fast. There was a bad one near Khalse where a
French woman had died.

    It was drizzling when we arrived. I made my way to
the Titse guest house. It was mellow and welcoming. The
proprietor family was lovely and the other travelers bright
and easy to talk with. I felt happy to be there. After a deep
sleep on my first bed off the ground in a month, I woke early
and did a long yoga workout. It was nice to have the space
to stretch and take my time. A bucket of water heated by an
electric coil freshened my body from head to toe. It felt nice
to be clean again. I joined the others for a long breakfast of

porridge and Indian tea and then set out, pack-free, into the streets. There were so many Westerners in bright, diverse clothes, catching to the eye like a circus event filled with lots of laughter and distraction.

Some tourists were kind and interested, but on the whole, they seemed so impatient and assertive to me, with little natural respect for other people. Their sense of cama- raderie was often based on cruelty, like the Frenchman who thought it humorous to hold his heavy-footed boot over a sleeping Ladakhi's head as if he would step on the old man taking a nap on the floor. My stomach turned, horrified and ashamed of my culture.

My time in the valley was sitting in me like an undi- gested meal. No one knew the adventures I'd been on, they saw me as just another hippy from Srinagar who had arrived in Leh by bus. For all the inner peaks and vales, the only ex- ternal evidence was the dust and leathered skin on my cheeks. Happy as I was to be in Leh, it was also hard to come back. I'd forgotten how civilization grated on my nerves, emptied my mind, and sapped my verve. I started running through the frames of my experiences over the last few days and what it felt like to be here.

From the vast open adventure, now I was just another face in another tourist town. The clergy ran a hotel, young monks threw a balloon around. My first cup of coffee went down, uneventful, after so many cups of salt tea. There was so much paper, tin, and plastic garbage on the street. And so much noise: sparrows, pigeons, running water, and a donkey braying below. Peace came with twilight, but my motivation was running low. It had been a long journey to get here. I had finally arrived, but where and to what, I wondered. Above the darkening sky, I couldn't see where I was headed without a guiding star. To catch the wonders of the earth, I had trav- eled quite far. But I couldn't take the peace I'd found, not the Zanskari's happy song. It can't be owned or held, it lived in that living current between us. So when I washed this body, the mountain dust removed, when I found the shoe man and patched my broken shoes, and when I finished all the business that seemed so pressing on the trail, what did I have left of the magnificent mountain way? The passes had left me breathless, so jagged and so deep, and the valleys between them, elephant-grey waters churning and icy sleet. What are these experiences? Are they imprints or something more? The Self that I'd been seeking leaves no mark, for it could never come or goes. If it was always present and never separate, who or what was there to take? If it was empty of any longing, then what hunger could I sate? What had I learned? I beseeched the air but the breeze refused to reply. What was I taking with me? What destiny had I?

A French woman passed by and startled me out of my thoughts; "You look like a Ladakhi!" She smiled and kept walking with a very French wiggle down the road. She had no idea how much that helped me at just the right moment. Or was she a dakini brushing by, leaving blessings in her wake?

I wanted to be with the Zanskaris I'd met but I'd left the valley and now I wore the label of a Western city girl. I didn't want to be a tourist, buying my way into the world, I wanted to be a pilgrim seeking out the real, not magic or myth but limitless bodhicitta and immeasurable bliss. Bodhidharma is said to have proclaimed, "The proudest creation is one's own character." He gave direct transmission, teaching no dependance on words and letters. See into the truth of your own nature. There is no salvation by formula. As awakened as they may be, Buddhas do but point the way. I was finding my way. The crossroads were just difficult to navigate.

There were so many soldiers in the area. Huge barracks sat at the edge of town with whitewashed stones lining the walkways with British precision. It seemed so out of place. The city was in a geopolitical hotspot. The border of India, Tibet, and China, with Russia just a stone's throw away, were all very interested in what happened in the region. But those forces had nothing to do with the way of life there; they didn't care what happened to the land, language, or people. Their goals weren't to create an enlightened society. The soldiers were always trying to strike up a conversation. They were probably lonely, so far from their big Indian families in some state far away. But I didn't like being around the military. Even though in India they'd be equally ready to talk about the nature of the Self, enlightenment, or philosophy, they were still in the context of force. The army was a good career for Indians, with respect, honor, and stability. I had the economic luxury to choose my profession and I'd always stayed away from the uniformed men.

In all of Zanskar, I saw no rule by force. What I did see were the fruits of following the rules of the bodhisattvas. The rules shaped character, laying the groundwork of enlightenment and bent the arc of culture towards wisdom. I learned what direction to circumambulate the mani walls, how to mark safe passage at a chorten with a rock, and the prayers that offered immeasurable riches through seven bowls filled with crystal clear water up to the width of one rice grain from the lip of the bowl—metaphors to inculcate in us a rhythm of altruism and aspiration. Giving generously, holding possessions and desires loosely, living with the truth of impermanence and the unspeakable freedom that is revealed when you let the background of consciousness come into the foreground of your mind.

When I visited the post office to buy some aerograms and flipped through the small packet of letters in the poste restante, I saw some names of travelers I'd met in other towns. It was a ritual on the backpacking circuit, seeing who might come through or names that become faces at some rest stop in the future. Few people knew I was there so I didn't search for anything for myself, just looked, connecting with the other seekers on the path. Then I saw familiar handwriting shaped into the letters of my own name. A friend from Dharamsala had forwarded it on to Leh, thinking I might pass that way if I was successful on my journey through the mountains, hoping it might arrive in time to connect with me the day after I left. What chance, what blessing. I smiled. In that world of misfits and adventurers, we took care of each other.

I went down to do some clothes washing by the river. The pounding on the rocks helped pacify my mind. I stopped for a quick chai at the Chang House when the heat lessened and the night began to fall. It was a full day and I felt happy. That night, I slept a deep sleep in a tent on the roof with Angmo, the proprietors' daughter, reading a copy of *Charlotte's Web*, the memories and associations that make us feel safe.

The week there passed in a bit of a blur, as often happens in travelers' guesthouses: Cooking, eating, getting over one illness or another. My stomach reacted to the dirty water, the microbes from so many tourists from so many different places. But towns had their advantages too. I wrote haikus while waiting in line at the bank and had a surprise reconnection with a German friend from my retreat at Koppan Monastery. So many different strands of myself, my interests, my life, my experiences, how to weave them all together? I loved having access to books again. There was a little library near the post office with a section of English books—Doris Lessing's *Martha Quest,* Aldous Huxley's *Island*, Robert Ludlum's *Road to Gandolfo,* D. H. Lawrence, Eudora Welty, George Orwell's *Burmese Days.* I devoured them one after another. But colonization was depressing, the roll of progress had a dark underbelly. It reminded me that I was in the middle of that too.

Though I'd been aware of advertising before, I felt, almost viscerally, how the messages put up on the walls throughout the city could plant thoughts in our minds, creating invisible norms and preferences. Like hardballs from left field, they pelted me. So many crowded messages in such small visual space: signs for guesthouses, skin whitening creams, Glucose biscuits, and powdered milk. The ways people from other countries dressed and moved through the streets were also advertisements for a different life. What a contrast to the stupas advertising the possibility of attaining Buddhahood in this very life. The mani walls advertised altruism, and the gompas of local stone and mud bricks set your mind on emptiness. The Zanskari wardrobe of one outfit of homespun wool, the same for men, women, children advertised contentedness, the quenching of the fires of desire. There was a closeness of fleeting life. The truth of karma, effects put into motion by actions good and bad, was evident. The valley went through short cycles of growth, two-month seasons for flowers and fields in mimicry of the short lifetimes of people, teaching us that when death comes it is time. No prolonging, no extension beyond natural means. Then the bodies were carried to high places and left for the vultures. Life was made up of simple elements, few choices, and few distractions. Stones, snow, water, wool, leather, and brass. Shoptsa, desert thorns, sweet incense of cinnamon roses.

I loved the magic and mystery. I was grateful for the people who had welcomed me in and cared for me. They had changed me. I was grateful for those mountains I felt so strongly for that it hurt. I couldn't change the karma I had come into this birth with, where I was born, or how I grew up. Wish as I might, I could not shed one culture to adopt another. Forging your own path is the hard way. Maybe that's how it always seems from the inside, even if you're within a tradition. The Buddha had to find his own way, wandering and trying things out. We all need to find our own way, whether that's following a structure or wandering from the feet of precious teachers to the lessons of the streets. I kept leaning into the questions, peering over the edge of the huge slope of not knowing into the deep valley of what would come next.

I talked with travelers, a girl from Berkeley College so nervous about the credits she was receiving for her time in Leh that she didn't seem to have realized the riches she was sitting in the middle of. That was the kind of education I had left at Cornell, learning for credits rather than character, for profession rather than purification, for income rather than illumination. We went on an easy walk through town and sat in a chang shop. The conversation veered towards colleges and paths of study. Everywhere you go, the traveler circuit attracts slightly different people. Leh was a magnet for bright, adventurous students who wanted to study and improve the world. In that way, their goals dovetailed well with the bodhisattva ideal to relieve sentient beings from suffering and help them reach enlightenment. The college students might not have thought in that context, but their ideals and considerations moved in that direction and the conversations were rich. In some ways, I felt not quite up to their speed. I guess I was a generalist, not focused on a single stream of research or study. In another way, it had always been the inner, the Being aspect, that had pulled me. I'd always felt that was my foundation, and anything of purpose would grow out of that. But their confidence made me doubt my choice to leave my education and live in India with an unstructured agenda.

Still, I figured earning wisdom and compassion came first, followed by whatever actions that became clear from that. I was learning, but not something that was easy to quantify or commodify to them. Putting myself in the hands of the mountains and people of Zanskar was softening me like pounding barley, their mortar and pestle generosity, happiness, and equanimity. I had never imagined a place where there was so much goodwill and harmony, where that was the norm, the currency of being. They brought me in without clinging, they accepted the crossing of our karmic paths without trying to get anything or hold onto me. Anyone could belong there and yet no one was attached. Life came and went, life into life with death as the transition, good deeds begetting a good life in the future, and care to live peacefully together generated harmony against the backdrop of the harshest of conditions. I never thought of Zanskaris as poor; their generosity was overflowing, in all the ways that were most important to me, they were vastly more rich than I.

The sun was so strong on the flat land around Leh that it was hard to do much in the middle of the day. At the guest house, everyone becomes old friends after exchanging names. We took kerosene stoves out into the courtyard and cooked together. Garath made a custard cake. Collin from New Zealand made sweet rolls and talked about the anthropology thesis she was writing. I made apricot jam from dried fruit I had bought from a Ladakhi woman in town. The fruits were dried right on the ground and little stones remained stuck to the wrinkled orange apricot flesh. We went from the guest house to the Chang House for a dinner of steamed momos and thukpa. The day passed, another transition day, a traveler's day, a re-entry day. I made plans to go by bus to the Choglamser Tibetan refugee camp with Carolyn and Martha who had been working there for the last eight months. As happy as the Zanskari seemed, they were on the border of China and a dangerous walk over snow mountains and treacherous passes. There is also a lot of recent suffering held by these people. Tibetans were still finding their way out of China and into India, some landing in Leh, hoping to preserve their language, religion, and way of life almost twenty-five years after the genocide. When the Chinese invaded Tibet in 1958, no one anticipated the brutal occupation that would follow. One sixth of the population died, over a million souls. Lamas and high rinpoches especially were singled out and tortured, humiliated, and imprisoned. Thousands of ancient sacred monasteries were destroyed, volumes and volumes of irreplaceable texts burned, jeweled statues looted, mantra carvings broken and used for latrines. Famine and resettlement followed, along with forbidding of Buddhist practice, worship, or familial support. This peace-driven people, who had lived by their practice for over a thousand years, was radically unprepared for the mechanized hostility. Refugees continued to stream into welcoming India, bringing with them the hardship and the scars.

I went to the refugee camp for a few hours. There was not much to do there unless you were part of an organization like my new friends were. The camp was more empty than I had expected and more regimented, with neat rows of simple buildings for those who had arrived with nothing and had to start a new life from scratch. I felt thoughtful, sad, and also relieved for what might become possible for these courageous few and for the eroding culture. A few international peacekeepers worked with them, a few Americans on loan from universities and a few medical personnel tending to frostbite and cataracts.

From the camp I continued on alone to Hemis, a graceful town with a magnificent monastery. There, a deep peace descended. Founded in the eleventh century, Hemis was large and beautiful, regal compared to the gompas tucked in the folds of the Zanskar Valley. It was said that

Nāropā, one of the most revered yogis in the Tibetan Buddhist schools, met his teacher Tilopa there. After completing twelve great trials and twelve "small" spiritual attainments, Nāropā attained the highest levels of the understanding of emptiness. An old biography of Tilopa, recounting his attainments, had been found in the monastery's library many years ago, making it a sacred pilgrimage point and an historic treasure. The devoted came from near and far. Hemis was also one of the main seats of the Drukpa Kagyu lineage. Every year, high lamas would come to perform special ceremonies and give teachings to the initiated so they could make progress on the path to the attainment of Buddhahood. The ancient and the contemporary mingled here. The weight of tradition and the effervescence of living practice.

I walked around the courtyards and small streets. I sat inside the gompa under the watchful eyes of Padmasambhava. Worlds blurred. The past and the present. The unknown future. Everything condensed into the most-pregnant moment of right now. My ankle stiffened and my foot numbed, pins and needles prickling my nerves. I was thirsty and a little stiff. The stilling of time roared in my ears. The crescendo seemed to rise from my heart. The moment was impossibly full. In that dusty dim gompa, the cells of reality were crackling and exploding with diamond-like beauty. A rain of love like lotus petals poured down onto my head. I looked around to see if it might be visible to anyone else. No, it didn't seem so. I was ok to keep sitting in my dark corner. People came and went. Monks set up offerings. Tourists moved in to inspect the thangkas more closely. Butter lamps smoked and cedar incense floated in from the doorway.

Emptiness is not a thing of the past or an attainment of the future. When the veils of illusion part, emptiness and perfection resound in all their splendor, irrespective of anything that has happened before or will happen afterwards. Happiness exploded in my body, a happiness that was different than a feeling or the result of an experience. Happiness as an essential condition or quality of Being was making itself known in my mind.

I was glued to my seat, a force as strong as whatever heaved the entire Himalayan range above the crust of the earth held me to my spot. There *is* nowhere to go and nothing to become. For an instant, I knew beyond any doubt no matter the struggles over how to fit in, what to do, where to live, how to actualize . . . none of it mattered. Angst was just another weather pattern crossing the unobstructed sky of awareness. Clear light, an immeasurable expanse of suchness always is, and is always free of blemish. My life, my questions, my apparent progress on the path was on one had real and must be well lived. Yet in essence, it is all part of the play, apparent movement on the surface of being, apparent shadow empty of substance, for there is no separate object to cast a shadow.

I heard a huge crack in my inner ear. Did that elder monk, whose rustling robes whooshed by me as he walked out the open temple doors, hear it too? The Tibetans say a loud snap happens at death when the consciousness bursts out of the body at the crown of the head, catapulting first to the bardo during a process of great transmigration, then into its next stage of existence. I wasn't dying, but in some way, I was. Some process was moving; my consciousness was escaping from the confines of limitation, bondage, separation. Like smoke that emits from a burning candle wick, no matter what happened next, it could never be put back. Gratefulness filled the cells of my body. I had no idea what this might mean for my life moving forward. In some quiet way that I couldn't explain, I felt that from a very young age, before I could remember, this was something I already knew.

May all beings everywhere
Plagued by sufferings of body and mind
Obtain an ocean of happiness and joy
By virtue of my merits.

For as long as space endures
And as long as living beings remain,
Until then may I too abide
To dispel the misery of the world.

SHANTIDEVA
(7TH—8TH CENTURY)

Glossary

Arsey: a lemony tasting grass-like vegetable.

Beyul: a secret heaven on earth, able to be revealed by adepts.

Bodhicitta: the desire to help all sentient beings be free from suffering.

Bodhisattva: an awakened one who forgoes Nirvana in order to help all sentient beings become free.

Bon: an ancient religion originating in Tibet, pre-dating Tibetan Buddhism.

Bonpo: a practitioner of Bon.

Chapatis: round flatbreads cooked on top of an open fire. (Hindi)

Chawal: rice. (Hindi)

Chortens: stone markers at the top of a mountain pass.

Dakini: female personification of enlightenment, associated with spaciousness and penetrating truth.

Dal: lentils. (Hindi)

Dhaba: restaurant. (Hindi)

Dorje: Tibetan ritual object.

Faran: Kashmiri wool tunic worn by men and women.

Gompa: Tibetan temple often connected to a monastery.

Gurgur: Tibetan tea mixer, a long cylinder with a plunger that blends salt and butter into the tea.

Indra's Net: a reference from the *Avatamsaka Sutra* (Flower Garland Sutra).

Jullay: Hello. (Zanskari)

Lila: the play or illusion of the world. (Sanskrit)

Kalpa: an aeon or very long time span, part of the cosmology of the forming of the universe. (Sanskrit)

Lung: winds or spiritual energy channels. (Tibetan)

Mahayana: one of the two main branches of Buddhism, developed in the 1st century BCE, that emphasizes dedicating one's practice to the awakening of all sentient beings.

Mala: Prayer beads, 108 on a string.

Mara: the personification of forces antagonistic to awakening.

Momos: Tibetan boiled, steamed, or fried stuffed dumplings.

Mudras: Ritual hand gestures.

Om mani padme hum: a common mantra recited to the Buddha of Compassion, named Avalokiteshvara (Sanskrit) or Chenrezig (Tibetan). Literally translated means, "Om! The jewel in the lotus."

Paba: Breakfast-like hot grain cereal.

Paramita: six qualities of an awakened heart, which include the perfection of generosity, ethics, patience, enthusiastic perseverance, concentration, and wisdom. (Sanskrit)

Perag: Zanskari women's jeweled headdress.

Pheran: Kashmiri-style wool coat.

Pikas: Himalayan gopher-like animals.

Pujas: Ritual prayers and ceremonies.

Sadhak: spiritual seeker.

Samskara: karmic imprints from previous lives.

Sho: yogurt.

Shoptsa: dried fenugreek, an aromatic herb.

Subji: Vegetable dish, also refers to edible spinach like greens.

Tapas: spiritual austerity.

Thangka: Tibetan Buddhist ritual paintings.

Tsampa: Dried and roasted barley flour, a staple food of Zanskar and Ladakh.

Thukpa: Soup with barley noodles, vegetables, or meat.

Tsog: ritual food offerings at a Buddhist ceremony.

Wheel of Becoming: a pictorial map of the basic tenets of Buddhism, including the stages of cyclic existence, the three poisons of desire, aversion, and ignorance, interdependence and impermanence, and the path to enlightenment.

Vajra: Tibetan Buddhist ritual object shaped like a lightning bolt, representing the capacity for profound and immediate transformation of consciousness. The contemplations it evokes in the practitioner include emptiness of all phenomenon, the non-separation of relative and absolute truth, the force and precision needed to dispel ignorance.

Vipassana: insight.

Zho: Yak-like animal.

Route

The following is the route I walked, grouped by segments or phases of the trek, which marked different stages of learning and being. Some of the town names have changed over the last four decades and some of my notes may be misunderstandings of the names I thought I heard. When I compared my 1983 travel log with contemporary maps, there were differences both in altitude and in village names. I did my best to resolve as many inconsistencies as possible, though differences remain. I chose to leave in some villages that aren't currently mapped, for I received their hospitality then. My apologies to those who make their homes in places I may have misnamed. The errors are only mine.

Kargil (2,650 m | 8,694 ft)
Following the west bank of the Suru River (Karcha Nar)
Sankyo
Namsuru (3,480 m | 11,417 ft)
Panikhar
Crossing the Karcha River
Suru
Pakarchik La
Walking to the west of Nun and Kun mountains and the Shafat Glacier
Jildo
Ringdom Gompa (3,667 m | 12,030 ft)
Tashi Tongse
Following the Sangpo River
Pensi La (4,400 m | 14,435 ft)
Walking to the west of the Drang Drung Glacier, *source of the* Doda River
Trakkur
Himling
Phe (3,505 m | 11,499 ft)
Tungri
Crossing the Stod River Sani Gompa
Padum
Walking along the Zanskar River
Karsha
Pishu
Crossing to the east side of the Zanskar River
Zangla

Crossing to the west side of the Zanskar River
Pishu
Pidmu Hanumil
Parfi La (3,950 m | 12,959 ft)
Snertse
Hanumil La (4,880 | 16,010 ft)
Chapskang La (4,200m | 13,779 ft)
Lingshet Gompa
Nietukse La (3,750 m | 12,303 ft)
Kupa La (3,870 m | 12,696 ft)
Singi La (5,060 m | 16,601 ft)
Bumiktse La (4,200 m | 13,779 ft)
Photoksar (4,200 m | 13,779 ft)
Sirsir La (4990 m | 16,371 ft)
Hanupatta (3780 m | 12,401 ft)
Wanla (3245 m | 10,646 ft)
Shilshil La (3726 m | 12,224 ft)
 Prikit La (3810 m | 12,500 ft)
Lamayuru
Leh
Chogslamer
Hemis

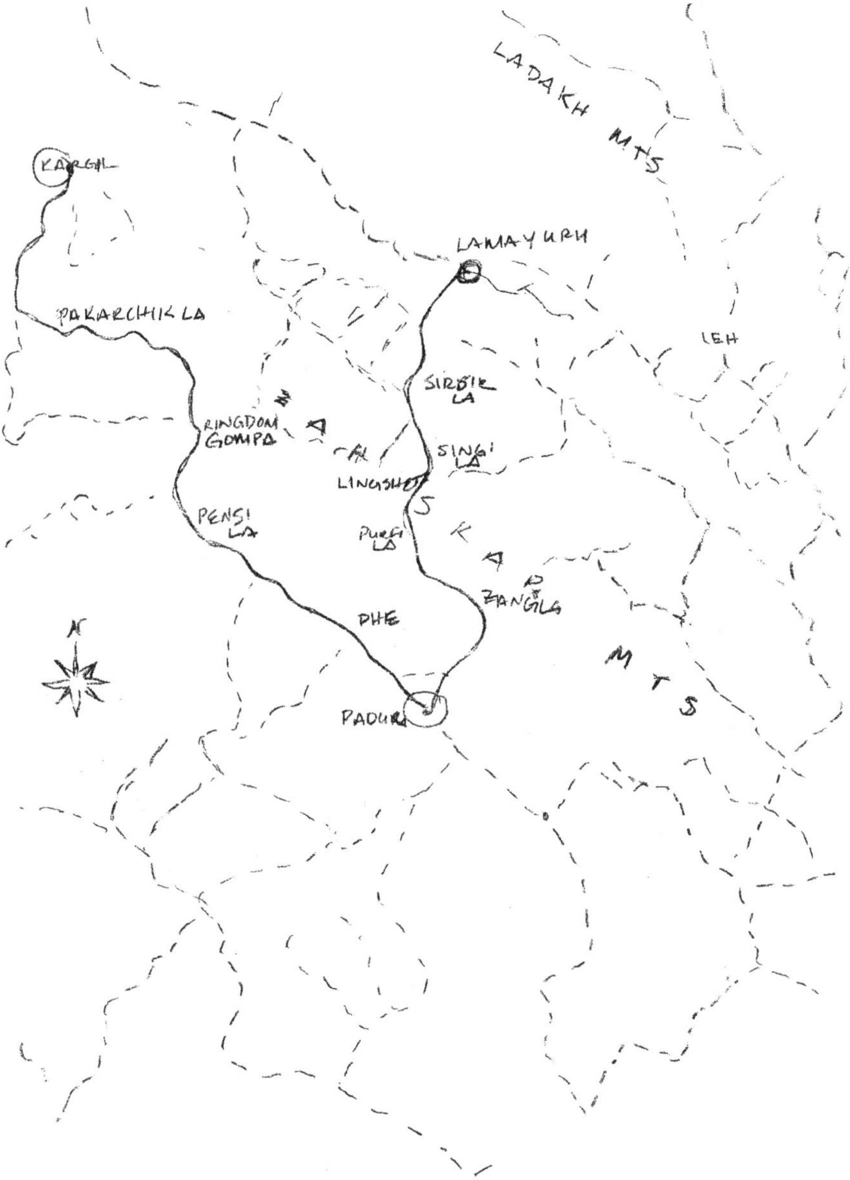

LADAKH MTS

KARGIL

PAKARCHIK LA

LAMAYURH

LEH

RINGDOM
GOMPA

SIRSIR
LA

LINGSHET

SINGI
LA

PENSI
LA

PURFI
LA

ZANGLA

DHE

MTS

PADUM

N

About Amy Edelstein

Amy Edelstein, educator, author, and nonprofit leader is a powerful communicator of ideas and beliefs that can help us transform ourselves and the culture we live in.

In 2014, Amy founded Inner Strength Education, a non-profit organization that has empowered thousands of Philadelphia teens in under-resourced schools with mindfulness and systems thinking tools. Amy began her own meditation practice in 1978, studying both Eastern and Western philosophies, and has been an avid practitioner of the contemplative arts ever since.

She is a Cornell University College Scholar in educational theory and cultural design. Amy was honored with a Philadelphia Social Innovation Award for her organization's work in Violence Reduction and her curriculum received the designation as a Collaborative for Academic Social and Emotional Learning (CASEL) recommended program. She is also author of six books including the IPPY award-winning, bestseller *The Conscious Classroom*.

More at www.InnerStrengthEducation.org

Quote Sources in Order of Appearance

Shantideva, Acharya. *A Guide to the Bodhisattva's Way of Life*. Translated by Stephen Batchelor. Library of Tibetan Works & Archives, 1988:v 75.

Aryasura, *Subhasita-ratna-karandaka-katha*: 16-18b; P5424: 235.4.3-5, from Je Tsongkhapa. *The Great Treatise on the Stages of the Path to Enlightenment*. Translated by the LamRim Chenmo Translation Committee, Joshua Cutler Editor-in-Chief, vol. 1, Snow Lion Publications, 2000: 123.

Tsongkhapa, Je. *The Twenty-Seven Verses of Mind Training*. *verse 14*, from Lex Hixon. *Mother of the Buddhas: Meditation on the Prajnaparamita Sutra*. Quest Books, 1993: 241.

Paldrön, Jetsun Mingyur. (1699-1769), from bka' gsang rdzogs pa chen po dkon mchog spyi 'dus khrid yig man ngag gsal sgron snying po published by D.G. Khochen Tulku, Mindroling Monastery, Clement Town, India, p. 17-18, from "Thought of the Week 32." *Matthieu Ricard*, https://www.matthieuricard. org/en/ thoughts/32. Accessed 2 Sept. 2021.

Buddha. *The Dhammapada: The Buddha's Path to Wisdom*. Verse 236, translated by Acharya Buddharakkhita. *Buddha Net*, http://www.buddhanet.net/pdf_file/ scrndhamma.pdf. Accessed 2 Sept. 2021.

Linpa, Jigme. (1729-1798). *The Treasury of Precious Qualities*. Chapter 7, verses 4-7. From "Thought of the Week 55." *Matthieu Ricard*, https://www. matthieuricard.org/en/ thoughts/55. Accessed 2 Sept. 2021.

Padmasambhava. *Guru Yoga*. From *Losang Samten*, https:// losangsamten.com/files/padmasambhava.pdf. Accessed 2 Sept.2021.

Buddha. *Tipitaka*, "Samyutta Nikaya," "Upaddha Sutta," Verse 45.

Dalai Lama, XIV, Tenzin Gyatso, *Oral Teachings given in Schvenedingen Germany, 1998* from "Thought of the Week 35." *Matthieu Ricard.* https://www. matthieuricard.org/en/ thoughts/35. Accessed 2 Sept. 2021.

Buddhaghosa, Bhadantācariya. *The Path of Purifications: Visuddhimagga.* Translated by Bhikkhu Ñānamoli. Pariyatti Publishing, 1991: 852-853.

Dalai Lama, XIV, Tenzin Gyatso, *Oral Teachings given in Toronto in 2004* from "Thought of the Week 46." *Matthieu Ricard.* https://www.matthieuricard.org/en/ thoughts/46. Accessed 2 Sept. 2021.

Tilopa. "Tilopa's Song to Naropa," from from Lex Hixon. *Mother of the Buddhas: Meditation on the Prajnaparamita Sutra.* Quest Books, 1993: 246-247.

"Prajnaparamita Sutras," from Lex Hixon. *Mother of the Buddhas: Meditation on the Prajnaparamita Sutra.* Quest Books, 1993: 29.

"Prajnaparamita Sutras," from Lex Hixon. *Mother of the Buddhas: Meditation on the Prajnaparamita Sutra.* Quest Books, 1993: 35.

Tilopa. "Tilopa's Song to Naropa," from from Lex Hixon. *Mother of the Buddhas: Meditation on the Prajnaparamita Sutra.* Quest Books, 1993: 246.

Buddha, *'Phags pa yongs su mya ngan las 'das pa chen po'i mdo, P787,: 147.3.5, 147.3.7-8. The Great Treatise on the Stages of the Path to Enlightenment.* Translated by the LamRim Chenmo Translation Committee, Joshua Cutler Editor-in-Chief, vol. 1, Snow Lion Publications, 2000: 147.

Palzangpo, Gendun Gyatso, The Second Dalai Lama. (1475-1542). Mullin, Glenn H., editor and translator. *The Second Dalai Lama: His Life and Teachings.* Snow Lion Publications, 1994: 164.

Shantideva, Acharya. *A Guide to the Bodhisattva's Way of Life.* Translated by Stephen Batchelor. Library of Tibetan Works & Archives, 1988: 103.

"Prajnaparamita Sutras," from Lex Hixon. *Mother of the Buddhas: Meditation on the Prajnaparamita Sutra.* Quest Books, 1993: 31.

"Prajnaparamita Sutras," from Lex Hixon. *Mother of the Buddhas: Meditation on the Prajnaparamita Sutra*. Quest Books, 1993: 39.

Bibliography

Govinda, Anagarika. *The Way of the White Clouds*. Overlook
   Press, 1966.
Heber, A. Reeve, and Kathleen M. Heber. *In Himalayan
   Tibet: A Record of 12 Years Spent in the Topsy-
   turvy Land of Lesser Tibet with a Description of its
   Cheery Folk, Their Ways & Religion, of the Rigours
   of the Climate & Beauties of the Country, its Fauna
   and Flora*. J. B. Lippincott, 1926.
Lal, P., translator. *The Dhammapada*. The Noonday Press,
   1967.
Muller, F. Max, translator and editor. "The Dhammapada:
   A Collection of Verses." *Full Books*, http://www.
   fullbooks.com/The-Dhammapada.html. Accessed 2
   Sept. 2021.
Ñānamoli, Bhikkhu, translator. *The Life of the Buddha
   According to the Pali Canon*. Pariyatti Publishing,
   1992.
Norberg-Hodge, Helena. *Ancient Futures: Learning from
   Ladakh*. Sierra Club Books, 1992.
Peissel, Michel. Zanskar: *The Hidden Kingdom*. E. P. Dutton,
   1979.
Rahula, Walpola. *What the Buddha Taught*. 2nd ed., Grove
   Press, 1974.
Ricard, Matthieu. *On the Path to Enlightenment: Heart
   Advice from the Great Tibetan Masters*. Shambhala,
   2013.
Stewart, Jampa Mackenzie. *The Life of Gampopa*. 2nd ed.,
   Snow Lion Publications, 2004.
Thurman, Robert A. F., translator. *The Holy Teaching of
   Vimalakīrti*. The Pennsylvania State University
   Press, 1986.
Tsongkhapa, Je. *The Great Treatise on the Stages of the
   Path to Enlightenment*. Translated by the Lamrim
   Chenmo Translation Committee, vol. 2 & 3, Snow
   Lion Publications, 2014.

Tsogyal, Yeshé. *The Life and Visions of Yeshé Tsogyal: The Autobiography of the Great Wisdom Queen.* Translated by Chönyi Drolma. Snow Lion Publications, 2017.

Yeshe, Lama Thubten. *The Bliss of Inner Fire: Heart Practice of the Six Yogas of Naropa.* Wisdom Publications, 1998.

Made in the USA
Las Vegas, NV
20 November 2021

34906207R00128